PEACE PIRATES

PEACE PIRATES

Conquering the Beliefs and
Behaviors that Steal Your
Treasure in Motherhood

ASHLEY WILLIS

Nashville New York

Unless otherwise noted, Scripture quotations are taken from the Holy Bible, New International Version®, NIV®. Copyright © 1973, 1978, 1984, 2011 by Biblica, Inc.™ Used by permission of Zondervan. All rights reserved worldwide. www.zondervan.com. The "NIV" and "New International Version" are trademarks registered in the United States Patent and Trademark Office by Biblica, Inc.™

Scripture quotations marked (NASB) are taken from the New American Standard Bible® (NASB). Copyright © 1960, 1962, 1963, 1968, 1971, 1972, 1973, 1975, 1977, 1995 by The Lockman Foundation. Used by permission. www.Lockman.org.

Scripture quotations marked (NKJV) are from New King James Version® Copyright © 1982 by Thomas Nelson. Used by permission. All rights reserved.

Scripture quotations marked (KJV) are taken from the King James Version of the Bible. Public domain.

Scripture quotations marked (ESV) are from the ESV® Bible (The Holy Bible, English Standard Version®), copyright © 2001 by Crossway, a publishing ministry of Good News Publishers. Used by permission. All rights reserved.

Scripture quotations marked (NLT) are taken from the Holy Bible, New Living Translation, copyright © 1996, 2004, 2015 by Tyndale House Foundation. Used by permission of Tyndale House Publishers, Inc., Carol Stream, Illinois 60188. All rights reserved.

FaithWords
Hachette Book Group
1290 Avenue of the Americas, New York, NY 10104
faithwords.com
twitter.com/faithwords

First Edition: April 2020

FaithWords is a division of Hachette Book Group, Inc. The FaithWords name and logo are trademarks of Hachette Book Group, Inc.

The publisher is not responsible for websites (or their content) that are not owned by the publisher.

The Hachette Speakers Bureau provides a wide range of authors for speaking events. To find out more, go to www.hachettespeakersbureau.com or call (866) 376-6591.

Library of Congress Cataloging-in-Publication Data has been applied for.

ISBN: 978-1-5460-1342-6 (hardcover); 978-1-5460-1341-9 (ebook)

Printed in the United States of America

LSC-C

10 9 8 7 6 5 4 3 2 1

CONTENTS

Part III: Treasure Up

PART I

Confessions of a Pirate Mom

CHAPTER ONE

Braving the Adventure

Key Principle: All moms must brave the various storms of motherhood, and they can experience peace through these storms when they choose to hold tightly to the Lord.

"I think the hardest part for me is always worrying if I'm forming my kids correctly. I want the best for them. I worry constantly about being too strict or not strict enough. I also worry about the example I set as a wife for my daughter and son. I so badly want them to have a wonderful Godly relationship."
—Kayleesue L., married with two girls and one boy

I will never forget the day when I thought I was officially losing my mind. And I don't mean it in the charming, "Oh, this crazy pregnancy brain" or "Man, there is so much on my plate these days" kind of way. I am talking downright cray-cray...or whatever young kids are calling it these days. I had no idea that rapper DMX was foreshadowing my future as a mother in his nineties hip-hop classic "Ya'll Gon' Make Me Lose My Mind (Up in Here, Up in Here)."

I was "acting a fool" with my four rambunctious boys more than I'd like to admit. And I will never forget when I realized that we were becoming a "ten-testicle home," as my husband loves to say. I seriously almost passed out when I saw yet another little baby penis on the ultrasound screen during my fourth pregnancy (and yes, I used the "p" word, which is most often the word of the day in my house). Between my boys' constant arguing, my requests that seemed to fall on deaf ears, and the older boys teaching my youngest an additional funny term for his genitalia, I was done.

I was so completely frustrated by the state of my position as mother and the behavior of my children that I found myself shutting down. I couldn't utter another pointless instruction or remind them for the four hundred and thirty-seventh time that we don't say, "Deez nutz!" at the top of our lungs in public (or anywhere else for that matter). Enough already!

Please don't misunderstand my candor, friend. I know it is a tremendous blessing to be a mother, and I thank God every day for my crazy kiddos. I just wish that the good *Little House on the Prairie* moments outweighed the bad *Roseanne* ones. Seriously! Not long ago my then-seventeen-month-old was dipping Oreos in the toilet and *eating them*, for crying out loud! The craziness is real, and some days—okay, most days—I feel in over my head. I feel like I've become a "pirate mom" just trying to navigate the raging seas of raising my precious little mateys, stealing chocolate from my kid's Halloween candy stash, barking off orders like it's my job, and bumping around the house in a sleep-deprived stupor until I gulp down enough coffee. Yeah. I may or may not have said, "Make haste, scallywag!" a time or two. Okay, it hasn't gone that far...yet.

Recently, my youngest sported a legit eye patch for months due to a lazy eye. Not to mention, my other boys are obsessed with pirate swords. We even dressed up like pirates for a Disney cruise with our extended family. My eldest son recently told me that he thinks I have an obsession with "pirate jackets," and you know, looking at my closet, I think there's a lot of truth to that statement. I mean, what's not to love about some lace-trimmed sleeves and military-style buttons adorning a blazer? I love it! So, yeah, we're pretty much a pirate family.

But in reality, pirates aren't fun or even fashionable. Pirates take from others. And when I allow myself to morph into a pirate mom—letting life toss me about like a ship at sea—I enable certain thoughts, circumstances, and people to plunder the peace in my heart and home. And consequently, our home becomes a topsy-turvy place lacking comfort, understanding, stillness, assurance, and most important, *peace.*

Our family spends a lot of long imaginative days at sea clanging plastic swords and finding buried treasure because it seems like the thing to do, but there are some days when I feel the heaviness of the playacting closing in on us. The reality of trying to steer clear of the chaos and avoid losing something valuable (like my mind!) throws us around—and it feels as if my peace and sanity are tossed overboard in the process. And I become even more pirate-y, if you know what I mean. Except I don't have an intimidating eye patch and my weapons aren't plastic pirate swords. My weapons come in the form of impatience, harsh words, eye rolls, frustration, and sighs toward the ones I love the most. I lash out—like a crazy pirate—at my precious little mateys. Then, I feel guilty, defeated, and depleted.

We're all emotionally seasick and desperately in search of the peace that was lost at sea. This is where *Peace Pirates* comes in. I want us to reclaim our hearts and our homes rather than giving them away to an elusive pirate that steals from us in the form of emotions, time, and other thief-like assaults on focus and frame of mind. Any other pirate mamas with me?

When I first became a mom, I envisioned my children challenging my authority on occasion, but I was sure they would be listening and following directions with a smile most of the time. I don't think any mom sits around daydreaming about her children running around half-naked and ignoring her instructions while burping the alphabet or begging their brothers and Dad to come look at their extra-long turdy in the toilet. Not what I expected at all. I wasn't prepared for the reality that I would nearly have to move Heaven and Earth to have some much-needed alone time with my husband to simply get on the same page and foster our relationship. I never thought this season of raising kids would be so hard!

I get so angry and frustrated sometimes because my role as a mother is nothing that I imagined and I feel completely out of sorts. I never imagined how shipwrecked and utterly helpless I would feel at times. I thought becoming a mom would make me better, not bitter. I thought it would make me grow, not grumble. Can you relate, Sweet Mama?

One night, I had more than I could take. I slipped into my bedroom and had one of those can't-breathe, mascara-all-over-the-face, ugly cries. My husband was so sweet to sit with me and rub my back as I let it all out. My kiddos happened to walk into the room and stared at me. I could see the thoughts swimming through their heads, like *Oh no! It's happening. Mommy is losing her mind!*

I just feel like I am missing *it* most of the time. You know? I have prayed for these kids since before they were born, and I continue to do so every single night. I have read countless parenting books on both child-rearing philosophy and practical correction advice. And yet I feel like I am not even running on fumes anymore. I have so many people in my life that I can lean on, including my amazing husband and mom, but I can't seem to shake this *feeling*. I love God, love my husband, and love my children, so why do I find myself missing out on the joys of motherhood so much of the time? Why do I feel like I have been pirated out of my peace, or worse, that I've become a pirate stealing affection away from my children? I certainly don't want my kids growing up with a mother who keeps something back due to anger or frustration. I don't want my emotions to ruin my marriage either. There is so much at stake, and I desperately want to get this right!

One aspect of our family that I have been determined to get right is our ability to work together as a team. Surely that can't be stolen from me, can it? I have so often admired those families in our lives who truly enjoy being together. They exhibit a kind of family togetherness that is inviting to all members of the family, young and old. My husband, Dave, and I desperately want this for our family, so a few years ago, we decided that we could cultivate this not only through prayer and daily interaction but also through taking on certain "adventures" as a family.

Most of our adventures have revolved around travel. We've become road warriors together, but sometimes it has felt like cruel and unusual punishment for all of us. After hours of driving, a few sweet moments of family singing, fights over gaming equipment, some impromptu games of "name that smell," and Dave and I saying, "If I have to stop this car..." like a broken record, we finally arrive at our destination completely exhausted. No matter how stressful the trip—which is now the expectation—we always seem glad we made the effort, and the memories do seem to bring us closer together as a family.

One year we decided to try a *new* kind of adventure. There was an absolutely beautiful canal in Augusta, Georgia, near our home, and Dave and I would often take long walks along the trail beside it. For years, I told Dave how much I would love to take our family on kayaks down the canal. He always looked at me funny when I mentioned it, but I finally convinced him that we should give it a try...even when I was thirty weeks pregnant with our fourth boy. Yeah. *Ahem.*

We were all dressed to go out for dinner, but we decided it was too gorgeous of a day to waste it indoors. So we took our boys to the canal to see the rapids and small waterfall. It was a perfect day: seventy degrees with a soft breeze and just enough crispness in the air to feel like fall when we stepped out of the sunlight. The boys loved seeing the rapids and were in great spirits. So Dave and I, intoxicated by the breathtaking sights and weather, decided to take the plunge.

We rented two tandem kayaks, put on our life jackets, and off we went on the four-and-a-half-mile, two-and-a-half-hour trek down the canal. No, I am not exaggerating those numbers, and yes, they were as daunting as they sound.

Without thinking of my growing pregnant belly, I decided it made the most sense for me to hold Chandler, our squirmy three-year-old, in my lap while trying to paddle in the back of one kayak. Meanwhile, we placed Connor, our quintessentially free-spirited middle son who refused to bring a paddle, at the front. Dave and our oldest, Cooper, each having his own paddle, were in the other kayak. Right before we pushed off from shore, our friendly rental agent told us we had better try to paddle the whole way down the canal or we would miss our shuttle back to our car, unless we wanted to paddle upstream in the dark. *Sure*, I thought. What could possibly go wrong? *Sigh.*

We started out on a pretty good trek. The weather

was amazing, and our kids seemed excited to experience something new. About ten minutes into the adventure, Chandler, our youngest, decided he wanted to move around the kayak at his leisure. If you have ever kayaked, you know that this is impossible unless you want to tip over. So I tried to calmly tell him to sit down and I even tried distracting him by pointing out an interesting bird on the water in front of us. He loved watching the bird, but he refused to sit down. I sharpened my tone a bit, insisting he sit down, because the kayak was shifting with his movement. Connor, the middle son at the front, thought our rocking kayak was hilarious, so he, too, began to move his hips back and forth to get the kayak rocking even more. My "what could possibly go wrong" attitude had been a bit presumptuous. I could feel my annoyance and frustration starting to mount.

Meanwhile, Dave and Cooper were oblivious to the catastrophe that was occurring in my kayak. They were paddling without a care in the world, pretty far ahead of us. At that point, I was getting desperate and could feel my blood boiling. Limited to a boat that was near tipping over with two kiddos, my pregnant self, and crumbling composure, I said loudly and obnoxiously, "I. Said. Stop. Moving. And. Sit. Down. *Now!*"

I might as well have said, "Or I am gonna throw you in myself!" from the look my youngest gave me. Yes, that's how classy this whole thing went down.

Chandler started crying uncontrollably, while Connor, feeling the awkwardness of the moment, started laughing like a hyena. Over by the trail, I could see a sweet, young couple strolling along and then stopping to gape at the crazy, tacky mother loudly reprimanding her kid in the middle of the canal. On a side note, I realized that I quite possibly might have made that young couple never want to have children. *Lord, please erase that scarring memory of a crazy mom from their minds.* Have mercy!

Finally, Dave and Cooper heard our clamor and began to paddle upstream to meet us. Dave could tell that I was spent and offered to turn us all around and head back. I, in my frustration and stubbornness, said, "No, we can't. We have been through too much and come too far to turn back now. We have to press on!"

So Dave, knowing that I was on the verge of tears with my raging pregnancy hormones and having only one paddle for our kayak, suggested that he tether our kayaks together. After all, we were cutting it really close to making it in time for our shuttle, and we certainly didn't want to paddle upstream in the dark. Dave found his inner "MacGyver" and creatively fastened the two kayaks together. And then he began paddling as fast as he could.

Knowing that he couldn't single-handedly get us there, even though he is some kind of Hercules in all of our eyes, he enthusiastically said, "Team Willis, I need all of you to help. Cooper, you've got to paddle, and Connor, you and Mommy can take turns with the paddle in your boat." So that's exactly what we did. It was hard work, but we found a way to make it to the end and even managed to take in the beautiful scenery around us without losing heart from our "adventure."

When we reached the finish line, we were all drenched

and exhausted, but there was such a feeling of accomplishment. We knew we could've given up, but we chose to press on. We knew we could've continued fighting, but we chose to get along. We knew we could've let our anger and frustration ruin our adventure, but we chose to change our attitudes (with me apologizing to my son for yelling) and enjoy this special experience together. That is what being a family is all about. We start together and finish together. We don't let anyone fall overboard or leave anyone behind. We are family, and we are on the same team, win or lose.

Although the kayak adventure was extremely difficult at times, and Dave now has tendonitis in his wrists to prove it, I would do it all again. I can now laugh at my frustration and appreciate the memories we made that day. It is all part of the adventures and sometimes *misadventures* of building family togetherness.

Do you sometimes feel like you and your family have more misadventures than real adventures? I used to believe the lie that I was the only wife and mom who dealt with this . . . until I started talking honestly about it and asking my friends about their own struggles at home. I was relieved to find out that we are *not* alone in our struggle. In fact, most moms deal with feeling that peace is lacking—and the fear that they are messing it all up—on a daily, if not hourly, basis. I take some comfort in that, don't you?

You see, I don't think it is any accident that you picked up this book. You, like me, long to be the mom God calls you to be, but many days, you're just not sure how that's supposed to happen. We go to church, we pray, we read the Bible, but we still have this sinking feeling that we are missing the mark—and anxiety steals our peace.

Sweet Mama, God didn't call us to live in defeat. Being a mom is hard, especially when you are navigating the rip-roaring seas of raising kids. This journey is difficult, but it is equally breathtaking in its finer moments. However, it's rarely smooth sailing.

The hard truth is we are all engaged in a battle, but it's *not* us against our kids. In fact, they are smack-dab in the middle of our ship with us, and all of us are holding on for dear life. This battle is a spiritual one. The enemy is ferociously trying to deplete us of our peace. I don't know about you, but I'm fed up with feeling defeated. I believe my God is greater than these "peace pirates": the negative influences that steal every ounce of peace from our hearts and homes and leave us feeling defeated and depleted. I know that *every* mom can learn how to thrive in these waters. We can and will defeat and stay ahead of these pesky peace pirates, but we can't fight them alone. And we certainly can't afford to turn into a pirate mom.

If you're like me, you feel a little guilty about getting frustrated or weighed down by the realities of it all. We tell ourselves things like, "My children are a blessing. Why can't I just stop stressing and enjoy this season?" Or, "Women have been moms for thousands of years. Why didn't anyone tell me how hard this was going to be?" Or, "Is there something wrong with me? It shouldn't be this hard, right?" Sound familiar, friend?

Here's what some real moms are saying about their struggle:

"I only really ever wanted to be a boy mom, but now I'm thinking a daughter who would profess her love for her momma might be nice! I love my boys so much, but what a difference it makes as mom of all girls (my BFF) and mom of boys & girls. My husband is so involved in our boys' lives as coaches in soccer, baseball, football, basketball, and golf that I sometimes feel left out or overlooked...or not respected for all I DO for the boys!"

—Larissa A., remarried with three boys

"Both of my children are under five and require tremendous amounts of attention and energy for keeping up with, training, supervising, and general care. Everything is new and unexpected. It is difficult to attend to other areas at the same time, such as cleaning and maintaining my home, work/projects/other commitments outside of home and marriage."

—Stephanie M., married with two kids

Friend, you are not alone in your struggle. This season is super hard. Don't be afraid to talk about it and go to God for help. He has and will continue to equip you to be the very best you can be when the daily storms are swirling around you. He will steer you in the right direction. And He can bring you the peace you so desperately need, especially as you parent.

God never promised us that we wouldn't be in rough waters, motherhood included. But he provided calm in the storm with the disciples and he'll do the same for us. Mark 4:35–39 describes Jesus calming a raging sea like this:

That day when evening came, he said to his disciples,
"Let us go over to the other side." Leaving the crowd
behind, they took him along, just as he was, in the
boat. There were also other boats with him. A furious
squall came up, and the waves broke over the boat,
so that it was nearly swamped. Jesus was in the stern,
sleeping on a cushion. The disciples woke him and
said to him, "Teacher, don't you care if we drown?"
He got up, rebuked the wind and said to the waves,
"Quiet! Be still!" Then the wind died down and it
was completely calm.

Have you ever felt "nearly swamped" in the raging seas
of raising kids? I know I have. The good news is that Jesus can and will calm the storms within our hearts and
homes just as He did for those in His company. He equips
us to brave the storm. He is our Prince of Peace, and
He can provide calm and peace through toddler temper
tantrums, potty training (isn't that just the worst?), behavior issues, academic struggles, teenage angst, teenage
relationship problems, back talk, slammed doors, and even
silent dinner tables. During all those moments that can
throw us overboard, pull us into the undercurrent, toss us
around, and drag us under, Jesus says, "Peace. Be Still!"—
sometimes to the moment itself, but mostly to our hearts.
God's Word confirms that we can do hard things. It is said
in 2 Corinthians 4:8–10, "We are afflicted in every way,
but not crushed; perplexed, but not driven to despair; per-
secuted, but not forsaken; struck down, but not destroyed;
always carrying in the body the death of Jesus, so that the

life of Jesus may also be manifested in our bodies." And Romans 8:37 states, "No, in all these things we are more than conquerors through him who loved us."

We don't have to live defeated. We don't have to let ourselves become hardened, yucky pirate moms who lash out. We don't have to simply "endure" motherhood. In fact, God made us for more than we think our own threshold is. God bestows one of the greatest callings a woman can have on a mother, and He will continue to equip us and restore our peace in the process. God certainly doesn't call us to be a mother at the expense of our relationship with Him.

In truth, one of the most basic ways we can know that we are following God's will for our lives is by accessing the level of peace in our hearts and homes. Peace is one of the Fruits of the Spirit that is evidence that we have the gift of the Holy Spirit through the acceptance of Jesus Christ as our Lord and Savior. Yet so many Christian mothers, including myself, have struggled to experience and hold on to His perfect peace day-to-day. Why is this?

Some days, I feel like I'm right in my sweet spot. I read my Bible and have a prayer time. My mind and heart are in the right place to face the day. And then—*Boom!*—one of my kids decides to be disrespectful. And my peace and, frankly, my sanity begin to waver. As much as I want to blame my little mateys for stealing my peace, I know that I can't. It has much more to do with the state of my heart than it does with my kids and their actions. There are certain "peace pirates" that I have allowed to get hold of me. Things like comparing my moments as a mom against someone else's, my desire to control, and unmet expectations leave me angry, frustrated, and disappointed with my life.

So how are we supposed to break out of this cycle? How do we take back our peace and keep the peace pirates at bay?

We will talk more extensively later in the book about what peace pirates are and how we handle them. It's important that we know we have more control over the things that steal our peace than we realize. We don't have to simply react. We can stay ahead of it when we have a better understanding of what tends to plunder our hearts and homes most.

When I was driving to pick up my older boys from school one day, I heard the Trace Adkins song "You're Gonna Miss This." It's one of those notorious country "cycle of life" songs about parenthood and how we should stop wishing away the tough moments. Honestly, in my more frustrating motherhood moments, I probably would've wanted to share some honest accounts with Mr. Adkins. However, in that moment, I felt like I needed to listen: "You're gonna wish these days hadn't gone by so fast... you're gonna miss this."

I used to think the song was sweet and kind of cheesy, but I think the message is one for all parents. We are not going to miss the arguments, messes, loud noises, back talk, or gross discoveries. And we probably won't miss having to do all the things for them that consume our days. Instead, when our kiddos are all grown up, we are going to miss those little things that we forgot to really take notice of: the spilling out of laughter that can't be contained, seeing pure and fearless joy deep within their eyes, big bear hugs from tiny arms that won't let go, watching your kids help each other when they don't think you are watching, the smell of the bathroom right after a big, messy bubble bath, your child saying, "I love you, Mommy," the smiles on their faces when they know they have done something great, and the feel of a sweaty head falling asleep on your chest and their soft, rhythmic breaths . . . to name just a few. I will miss *all* of these moments. These are the real treasures in my life that no person or circumstance or peace pirate can take away from me. As a pirate mom striving to steer my family toward peace, I can use my skills to take the best of these moments, to actively hunt for these treasures, and hide them in my heart so I can cherish them forever.

As I was writing this chapter, my eldest son, Cooper, peeked over my shoulder and saw the part title. He laughed and asked, " 'Confessions of a Pirate Mom'?"

"Don't you think Mommy is kind of like a pirate sometimes?" I said.

"Yeah . . . no, not really," he said sarcastically, and gave me a big smile and a hug.

Little did he know . . . but this pirate mom was taking his little golden nugget of a reaction straight to my treasure chest.

As Cooper walked upstairs to bed, I couldn't help but think that maybe I'm not losing it after all. Maybe I just need to scoop up and savor the many golden nugget moments happening all around me during all the different phases of raising our boys. It's all around me for the taking, and Sweet Mama, it's all around you, too. So let's go after it!

We are not promised a life without frustration or hard times, but even so, God calls us to pursue peace and seek joy in all circumstances, regardless of our feelings. Friend, it is my hope and prayer that as you read this book, you will experience more peace and joy in your heart and home. Get ready, Brave Mama! We're going after those peace pirates with everything we've got.

Let's kick it off with a prayer for pirate moms everywhere:

Lord, help me to find pockets of peace today. I pray that I won't just endure raising my kids, but instead I'll truly enjoy them. I pray that I will have a heart that is open and eyes to see the good moments when they happen. Help me to hold on to these golden times. Calm the anxiety inside me and help me to remember that I have been blessed with these children. Encourage me with the truth that you give me strength to brave the adventures with my kids—even the squalls that come with motherhood.

In Jesus' name,
Amen

CHAPTER TWO

Shipwrecked

Key Principle: God uses our shipwrecked moments of motherhood for His glory and our growth.

"As a mom, I don't feel like enough is getting done (not enough hours in the day), kids are misbehaving, and I'm at a loss as to what to do with a raging testosterone sixteen-year-old boy. . . . And we just found out I'm six weeks pregnant . . . big sigh."

—Monica H., remarried mom of two

I love water. I think it's breathtakingly beautiful, especially when it sparkles in the sun. I love to swim in it, drink it, and use it to clean. Water is essential to life as we know it. But as much as I like to look at water and use it all day long, I'm not a huge fan of sailing on a boat—unless it's a huge cruise ship because, well, it's a cruise. When it comes to smaller boats, I'm not too keen to get in. I'll try it. I'll even tell myself it will be fun. But every time, I end up getting motion sickness.

So when I first read about the apostle Paul's shipwreck on Malta, all I could think about was how sick and scared everyone must have been before they finally reached the shore. Not to mention, Paul was traveling on this ship as a prisoner. In Acts 27:13–20, Luke, a physician and the author of the Gospel of Luke, records the event like this:

When a gentle south wind began to blow, they saw their opportunity; so they weighed anchor and sailed along the shore of Crete. Before very long, a wind of hurricane force, called the Northeaster, swept down from the island. The ship was caught by the storm and could not head into the wind; so we gave way to it and were driven along. As we passed to the lee of a small island called Cauda, we were hardly able to make the lifeboat secure, so the men hoisted it aboard. Then they passed ropes under the ship itself to hold it together. Because they were afraid they would run aground on the sandbars of Syrtis, they lowered the sea anchor and let the ship be driven along. We took such a violent battering from the storm that the next day they began to throw the cargo overboard. On the third day, they threw the ship's tackle overboard with their own hands. When neither sun nor stars appeared for many days and the storm continued raging, we finally gave up all hope of being saved.

I can't imagine how awful that must have been. Can you? Hundreds of men. Sick. Afraid. Hungry. Wet. Exhausted. In the middle of the ocean. Throwing supplies and gear overboard to secure themselves onboard. Ship falling apart at the seams. For days and days with no end in sight! It is no wonder that they were all losing hope of being saved. But the story doesn't end there. As Luke continues to recall the events, he describes how Paul, still a prisoner on this ship at the time and just as exhausted as the rest, stood before these weary men and told them about an angel of the Lord staying beside him through the storm and comforting him. This angel told Paul not to be afraid and said God would bring all of them to where they needed to go and none would perish. At the end of his encouraging words, Paul said, "So keep up your courage, men, for I have faith in God that it will happen just as he told me. *Nevertheless*, we must run aground on *some island*" (Acts 27:25–26, emphasis mine).

Oh, how I love how very human Paul is in his reaction. Yes, he chose courage and faith in the Lord. Yes, he chose to encourage the other men as well. Even still, I can sense his frustration. And honestly, why wouldn't he be frustrated? He knows that God is going to get him where he must go, but God didn't put an easy path before them. I'm sure Paul asked God why He allowed him to be a prisoner, why He made him go through this long, terrible, sickening storm, and why He wanted them to be shipwrecked on "some island." If I'm honest, I know I would have had all those questions and more. So, I get the tinge of exasperation in his words.

I'm going to come back to this story in a moment, but I want us to pause here for a few minutes and think about how this is quite like where we find ourselves in motherhood so much of the time. Sweet Mama, have you ever felt like your heart (and sanity, for that matter) is being tossed around like the men were on this ship? I have. Maybe you have, too. I know that God gave me the precious people on my mothership (wink, wink) for this season and for a greater purpose, yet the day-to-day chaos, strain, misunderstanding, frustration, exhaustion— and on and on—hit me like the raging and relentless storm those men experienced on the ship. And just like the weary sailors on that ship, I feel like I have to start tossing stuff overboard to level out my environment, be- cause deep in my heart, I know I am heading for a shipwreck. Utterly consumed by my emotions and ex- haustion, I make snap judgments and end up throwing out the very "stuff" that I *need* to make it through the storm in one piece. Things like good sleep, quiet time with the Lord, a cup of coffee with a good friend, a sweet embrace from my husband, and snuggles with my kids at the end of the day—things that promote and protect the *peace* in my heart and home.

In a desperate attempt to regain my composure and san- ity, I become more exposed and vulnerable than ever to the pesky minions who want to steal the little peace I have left—the peace pirates. And fear sets in because I know that I am fresh out of ammo, armor, and energy. I am done. I allow the peace pirates to hold up their threatening swords at me and hold me down in fear. I listen to their nasty, degrading words that shame me and make me feel like a failure as a mother. "This is all *your* fault, Ashley! How could you let it get this bad? You don't know what you're doing, and you're a terrible mother, wife, friend, daughter, worker, etc." Their callous words are like daggers in my heart, and I emotionally bleed out and surrender to the numbness that I feel. As my shell of a mothership eventually crashes into the shore, I am spit out onto the sand, holding my precious people tightly, but feeling lost, confused, and ashamed.

Thankfully, this shipwreck doesn't have to be the end of my adventure. Just as with Paul and the soldiers on his ship, God can use my shipwreck moments for my good, the good of others, and ultimately for His glory. There is a certain maturity and perspective that can be gained only from being shipwrecked by life. You might be reading this and thinking, *Does God really* cause *us to be shipwrecked or does He simply* allow *us to be shipwrecked?* The answer to both questions is "Yes."

In Luke's recounting of Paul's shipwreck as recorded in Acts, he states that Paul said an angel came to him to comfort him and assure him that he and everyone else on the ship would be okay. However, the angel also told him that they wouldn't have smooth sailing to their destination. As Paul put it, they must "run aground on some island." Friends, God was in control throughout this whole storm, and this is clearly evident because He sent an angel to be with Paul. He didn't want him to be afraid or feel alone. How awesome is our God! What's even more amazing is that He gave Paul an inkling of what he would initially

perceive as a diversion in their course. Even so, Paul chose
to trust God and inform and comfort the other men with
what he had learned. And what happened on that island
was not what Paul expected. In Acts 28, we learn that
the ship did indeed become shipwrecked on the island of
Malta. And after some interesting circumstances, Paul was
called to the chief official's home. The chief official, Pub-
lius, was suffering from dysentery and in desperate need of
healing. Paul placed his hands on him and healed him, and
then all the sick people on the island heard of the healing, came to see Paul, and received a miraculous healing as
well. Isn't that amazing? They ended up staying on Malta
for three months, and the people there were gracious to
them and supplied them with everything they needed to
set sail to Rome.

I think this story has a lot to say about peace in the
midst of hard circumstances. Just like Paul, we can walk
closely with the Lord and have a clear understanding of
His calling in our lives. For Paul, it was Rome. He knew
that was where God was telling him to go. But I'm sure
he never thought he would sail there as a prisoner on a
ship full of angry, weary soldiers weathering a two-week-
long, heinous storm leading to a shipwreck on a remote
island where they would heal the sick and stay for three
months before, once again, striving for Rome. Nope. I'm
pretty sure that wasn't anywhere on his radar. But God
rarely takes us on a predictable or easy journey.

Rome probably isn't the place where God is calling you
and your family—or maybe it is...and can I come, too?
Maybe you know that God is calling you to homeschool

your kids, or start a new business, or move your family to another country to be missionaries, or start a blog, or begin doing devotionals with your kids in the mornings, or join a Bible study, or...you name it. Whether a big decision or small, God is calling each one of us to an adventure as we grow in our relationship with Jesus, do our best to love those He has placed in our homes and lives, and discern and live out His will. It will be full of twists and turns, ups and downs, and everything in between. But through it all, whether our sails are tattered from storms, or whether we've been thrown off course and shipwrecked, God is still in control. He is with us. Comforting us. Encouraging us. Loving us. Giving us peace. A peace that surpasses our own understanding (Phil. 4:7). Knowing Him and knowing that He is truly with us through the hardest times brings us peace.

Then there's fear. Fear is a force of nature striving to wreak havoc in our lives and take our eyes off God—our only constant source of peace. It's paralyzing, confusing, and energy zapping. Fear comes at us like an unexpected, gigantic, and ferocious wave; once we feel the darkness of its shadow looming over us, it chokes out the courage in our hearts. Our minds become filled with racing thoughts of "what if," and worry begins to weigh us down.

A lot of people online use the acronym "FOMO," or Fear of Missing Out. As a mom, I struggle with some FOMO, but not as it relates to what my friends are doing together based on the fun photos they post and share. My FOMO has to do with the fleeting moments that take place all around me every day. Deep in my heart, I fear that

I am going to miss out on the precious moments that God has given me with my kids.

No matter where we go or what we do, we can't escape it. Time. It's constantly ticking away. We're early. We're late. We say things like, "You're ahead of your time," and "Get with the times." It's a constant reality for all of us. We've been getting older since the day we were conceived, but it's hard to notice how *we* are changing when we're in the midst of it. I think we become even more aware of time once we're raising and teaching children—we watch time aggressively tick away one milestone, one birthday, one boo-boo, one graduation, and even one pet burial at a time.

I tend to be a bit of what my parents would often refer to as a "worrywart." I'm not quite sure who first came up with that expression, but nevertheless, it doesn't make the act of worrying seem very attractive. I used to think that the fact that I worried about someone or something meant that I *cared* more. The older and, hopefully, wiser I get, the more I realize this couldn't be further from the truth. Jesus said, "So don't worry about tomorrow, for tomorrow will bring its own worries. Today's trouble is enough for today" (Matt. 6:34 NLT). Worry can be overwhelming and paralyzing in our lives. I have known people who will not leave their homes because of their worries. I see marriages stay in a catatonic state for years because of the worries of one or both partners.

When I read Matthew 6:34, it is clear to me that Jesus is telling us we cannot withstand the worries of yesterday or tomorrow. God has given us the strength to deal with only those challenges we will face today. On the surface, this may not seem very significant. But if you can grasp it, it will free you! It means that we don't need to be controlled by the worries of our past or our future. Instead, we need to have a laser focus on what is at hand today. That's enough. We don't need to do more than that. I don't think Jesus is telling us to forget about yesterday completely or not to make plans for the future; He is just telling us not to *worry* about it. There is a big difference between thinking about something and worrying about it. In fact, whenever worry fills our minds, we need to refocus our thoughts on the good things that fill us with strength. Philippians 4:8 states this beautifully: "And now, dear brothers and sisters, one final thing. Fix your thoughts on what is true, and honorable, and right, and pure, and lovely, and admirable. Think about things that are excellent and worthy of praise" (NLT). And more than that, God will help us conquer whatever we may face in this day. Now that's good news!

My husband, Dave, has always encouraged me to *flee* from worry. A while back he read a passage from Martin Luther, and shared a wonderful word picture with me that has truly changed the way I look at worrying and the thought process that leads me there. Luther said that if we picture our mind as a tree, then we can consider our thoughts to be like birds. Many birds (our thoughts) will fly over or around our tree (our mind) but we don't have to allow the birds to make a nest there. In other words, we are the gatekeepers of what we allow to dwell in our mind. I am sure you have heard Proverbs 23:7, "For as he thinks within himself, so he is" (NASB). We can so often become what we think about the most, which means we have to be conscious of what we allow to take up residence in our minds.

There was a time at the beginning of my marriage when I allowed too many worries to build a nest in my brain. Some days, I truly found it hard to breathe without having a nervous feeling in the pit of my stomach and nausea, just from the weight of the worry. I couldn't make a continuous inhale and exhale without flinching and then gasping for air. It was exhausting and crushing. For four years, I found myself in a full-fledged depression that I just couldn't shake on my own. I knew I needed help. I felt emotionally and mentally shipwrecked. Every day, I would wake up and feel "normal" for a minute or two, but then sinking feelings would creep in like hands trying to tear through my stomach just to get a choke-hold on my heart. There were days I was so riddled with anxious thoughts and sadness that I couldn't even remember what it felt like to have peace. I felt shipwrecked on a desolate island all by myself with ferocious waves on all sides. No way out. No friendly ships coming to the rescue. Just me and my disparaging and worrisome thoughts.

I felt ashamed and full of self-hatred because I was convinced that I must have done something wrong to feel the way I felt. I was damaged. I told myself that I probably wasn't believing in Jesus enough, or praying enough, or worshipping enough. I thought I was a terrible wife and mother. There were even days when I wondered if my family might be better off without me—a shell of the person I once was: *disengaged, sad, anxious, damaged.*

But that was not the end of my story, thank You, Lord Jesus!

Even on my lowest days, I could still hear God whispering messages of love and hope to me. I felt His presence with me. I cried out to Him constantly for help. He was with me every step of the way. He never left me on that island, and I knew that in His time, we would leave the island of anxiety and depression *together.* My peace—His peace that surpasses all understanding—would be restored. You see, the enemy had others plans for me. He tried to convince me that my thoughts should be my compass, instead of the Lord Himself. He wanted to knock me down, beat me up, break up my family, and fill me with shame. But our Father never leaves His beloved children in our despair. He picks us up, holds us tightly, cleans up our wounds and mends them, heals our hearts and relationships, and takes our hand and leads us to where we need to go. He is with us and for us—always.

Through years of prayer, the support of my husband (and eventually family and friends), reading lots of books, focusing on God's promises in His Word, watching hours of Christian television until late into the night, and Christian counseling, I was able to rid my brain of all those worrisome nests slowly but surely. Though it was many years ago, I will never forget the feeling of freedom I received each time I let my worries of the past and future go. God gave me peace that surpassed my understanding and helped me to bravely face each day in the midst of one of the hardest trials of my life, and I never want to forget that. Friend, He can do that for you, too. You don't have to live a life feeling defeated and depleted. You can have His perfect peace as you bravely and boldly face each day.

Over one spring break, Dave and I and our four boys met up with some dear friends of ours at an amusement park. With the age split of our children, Dave decided to take the older kids on some roller coasters, while my sweet friend Lana and I took the little ones to the playground area. On our way there, my then-four-year-old, Chandler, spotted a walkway with a huge red sign that read, WATCH OUT. SPLASH ZONE—not exactly *my* idea of fun. Chandler couldn't read very well at the time, but I could see his little mind trying to figure out why the sign was there. About a minute later, a roller coaster car whooshed down and slid through a small body of water nearby. The impending splash came roaring toward us. Chandler's eyes were wide, and his grin slowly grew until you could see every tooth in his smile. I hadn't packed swimsuits or towels, so I grabbed Chandler, and my friend pushed the stroller, as we quickly got out of the way.

Chandler laughed as he watched a few "big" kids get soaked. I told him to come along so we could go to the playground for kids his age, but he just stood there and waited for the next splash in his best Superman stance while gradually edging closer and closer to the biggest splash zone. Normally, his unwillingness to follow directions would anger me, but he was so excited, so brave, so cavalier and ready to withstand the big splash, that I figured, *Why not?* I chose to stay in the dry area with the baby and my friend . . . putting myself in a position to have a good view of Chandler from afar.

I had my cell phone ready to capture the moment, but part of me was dreading the tantrum that I was certain Chandler would have after getting soaked by a sudden harsh wave of water. But that *look*—that bravery and excitement in his eyes—made me want to give this, and him, a chance. So I did.

Soon, we heard the screech of the oncoming roller coaster and the high-pitched screams of the passengers as they took a sharp turn into the water. Chandler was unscathed by it all. In fact, he positioned himself right in the middle of the biggest splash zone—feet planted, glimmer in his eyes, shoulders back, and smiling ear to ear. Right before the splash, he looked back at me with his eyebrows raised and yelled, "Mom! It's coming!" Before I could answer him . . . *splash!* He was drenched with water to the point I worried about his little body being knocked down by it all. When the splash droplets cleared a bit, I could see a few kids running to their parents crying, and a few angry parents running away with them and shaking their heads at themselves for missing the big red sign. Then, right there in the middle of it all—with no one beside him—I saw Chandler. I snapped a picture right before he started walking my way while attempting to wring out his shirt. "That was *awesome*, Mom," he said. "I want to do it again! But next time I want you to come with me."

He must've seen the apprehensive look in my eyes, because he grabbed my hand and said, "Be brave, Mommy. I will be with you."

How could I say no to that?

I was so proud of my little man for being so brave, and I wanted to show him that Mommy could be brave, too. However, in all honesty, I didn't want to get wet right then and there. All I could think about was how uncomfortable I might be the rest of the day and how I didn't have an extra pair of shoes and dry clothes with me. Yet there he was looking up at me all bright-eyed and bushy-tailed and simply wanting me—*me*—to experience the big splash with him.

I looked at my friend. Quickly she said, "Go ahead! I'll stay with the baby." I asked her if she was sure she didn't mind, and I saw that the baby was starting to fuss a bit. Just as I began to decline Chandler's request, I stopped myself. I felt God nudging me and saying, *Go ahead, Ashley! You don't want to miss this.* So I took Chandler's hand, and we walked over to the soaking area and waited. We soon heard the roller coaster car coming toward the water and braced ourselves to be immersed. The water hit us like a tidal wave, and big, fat droplets were all around us. Chandler clung tightly to me and squealed with delight. We were completely soaked...shoes and all. He laughed hysterically when he saw how drenched I was. I couldn't help but laugh, too. We were a mess with squishy shoes and sopping wet clothes, but we had a blast together.

Later, as we continued to walk around the amusement park, it hit me—how many "splash zone experiences" had I missed with my kids? How many times had I turned my kids down because I didn't want to "get wet"? How many times had I been so task-oriented that I failed to immerse myself in the goodness, innocence, and sticky-sweetness of their childhood? If I'm honest, I'd have to say I've missed a lot of those moments.

Now, don't get me wrong here. I've been *there*. I've been present watching from the sidelines and cheering them on—all good things. However, there have been many times when my sweet kiddos have begged me to do more than just watch them—wanting me to experience the joy of playing with them—and I have failed to see the value in it. I've told myself all the reasons why I'm too busy to stop and play. I mean, I've got things to do, right? I've got to do laundry, help with homework, run children here and there, get my work done, make calls, answer e-mails, and find time to engage with my sweet husband, too. I've got my *list*, and most days, I'm just too busy to play for long . . . if at all.

Can you relate, Sweet Mama? Have you been there, too? I say all this not to make myself or anyone else feel bad, but to remind us all that childhood is a fleeting season that we don't want to miss. Let's not be afraid to get wet, dig in the dirt, and be dripping with sweat. Let's engage in play *more* than we watch from the sidelines. There are only so many years when they actually think we're cool enough to participate anyway. And when we do, we'll experience the real magic of childhood through their eyes. Let's not miss out on this amazing gift. Be brave, Mom. Be brave. Even when you feel apprehensive. Even when you're tired. Even when you feel shipwrecked.

A prayer for the mom who feels shipwrecked:

Dear Lord,

I am tired and weary today. I love being a mom, but there are so many days when I'm overwhelmed by all the tasks I need to complete, the worry I have for my children, and the frustration I feel with myself when it seems as if I've somehow missed the mark and the destination that You are leading me to. Remind me that there are times You allow us to be shipwrecked for a season for our growth and Your glory. Help me to remember that You never give me more than I can bear with Your help. I recognize that I desperately need Your help to be the peace-filled mother that You want me to be. Give me glimpses of You using these hard seasons to help me grow closer to You. I know You are with me and for me, Lord. Even when I feel shipwrecked and helpless, You are right there by my side holding me, calming me, and encouraging me. Thank You, Lord! May I surrender more and more to You every day, and may my heart and home be filled with Your perfect peace that surpasses understanding.

In Jesus' name,
Amen

CHAPTER THREE

Walking the Plank

Key Principle: God is much more concerned with our peacefulness as a mother than He is with our performance as a mother.

"As a mom, I am most stressed out at night. I'm usually prepping for the next day's challenges, whatever those may be, and after all the prep I sit down and plan/worry about what I need to do. This often carries over into bed unless I'm really tired. But when morning comes, the plans get carried out and stress comes, too, while [I am] trying to get everything accomplished and [am] being pulled in every direction."

—J. Loop, married mother of two

You started the day with a plan. You had your coffee, spent a little quiet time in the Word (okay a couple min-

utes, but still...it was something). You got the kiddos
dressed and ready to face a bright and shining new day.
You told them your expectations, like "When we go to an
office, we use our inside voices."

You got everyone into your awesome minivan and went
to your first task of the day—the orthodontist. You shuf-
fled everyone in there and found a cluster of seats to fit
your whole brood, sent off the one who was there for the
doc, and gave the littles a healthy snack that you'd gathered that morning and wisely placed in the diaper bag. You
even got out devices to allow them to play a few games
while waiting on their sibling. This was a special treat, so
you were sure it would make things go smoothly. And it
seemed to be working.

Ahhhh...you exhaled as everyone seemed to be occupied
and you got out that book you've been waiting for months
to read when all of a sudden...everything fell apart.

Maybe it was the baby screaming, or the toddler whining
profusely for the other device that his brother had, or the
food flying through the air from the upset baby who was
still crying—because you were busy tending to the whiny
toddler. Maybe it was the whiny toddler huffing and puff-
ing and squealing loudly when you placed him in time-out
and took away his electronic device, until you finally had to
physically pick up your toddler in one arm while pushing
the baby in the double stroller through the waiting room,
the entrance, and the bathroom doorway while bumping
into every other seat and saying, "I'm sorry," over and over
to the nervous onlookers. Maybe it was the fact that said
toddler screamed at the top of his lungs in the bathroom—

creating a bloodcurdling echo for everyone to hear—while someone else anxiously knocked on the bathroom door and the baby started to cry because the whiny toddler had decided to be extra strong-willed today. Maybe it was the ten minutes it took for you to finally get your whiny toddler to listen and calm down—for two minutes.

Or maybe it was *you*. It may have been the stares you felt directed at you. It may have been the crazy feeling rising up in you every time your kids blatantly disobeyed and refused to listen—and it just made you want to scream. But when you did raise your voice, you felt guilty and terrible inside. So you apologized, and hugged and kissed them, breathing relief in their forgiveness for a moment. But then they repeated the same frustrating things again the next hour or day. You found yourself fantasizing about being in a solitary room for a few hours where no one would want or need anything from you, and any request you had was obeyed *the first time* with no back talk or discontent. *Sigh*.

It may have been the embarrassment you felt inside because "good kids"—kids who listen to their parents and don't whine and don't have to be told something more than once—don't act that way. After all, yours wouldn't act that way if *you* were a "good parent." At least that's what you tell yourself in stressful moments.

As you sat in the waiting room wondering why in the world this appointment was taking so long, you finally had a few minutes to read your book—another book about parenting to add to the twenty other books you've read about parenting. Tears filled your eyes as you read the title of this particular book—*You're Kid Is a Brat, and It's All Your Fault*. How fitting for a moment like this, right? It *was* your fault, right?

Wrong. Dead wrong, Sweet Mama.

Sure, you've made mistakes like every other parent from the dawn of time, but you can't blame yourself for every little thing your kids do wrong. Sometimes, kids don't listen. They mess up like we do. Over and over and over again. So what do you do in these stressful, embarrassing, heart-pumping, frustrating moments? You do what *you* can do. You stay as consistent as you can and follow through. You do the very best you can every single day. You are trying your best here, and trying your best as a parent is super hard some days.

Have you ever lost your mind in the presence of your kids *because* of your kids? You know...you're doing your best to maintain your sanity, but stress takes over and you begin talking to your kids with a crazy kind of intensity, dragon-like nostrils (minus the smoke) and eyes that could slice like a knife? Well, I joined those ranks one night a few years ago. I am not proud of this at all, but I want to be real with you, friend.

It all started when the boys and I decided to get our friend a get-well gift. Sweet, right? So we set out for the get-well gift gallery—the Dollar Tree, of course. The boys were a little riled up in the car and a touch argumentative, but nothing too out of our norm. So we parked the car and burst into the store with glee and started looking at gift items.

My middle son, Connor, was wearing his brand-new prescription glasses, which he'd gotten just the day before.

He was extra hyper, bouncing from aisle to aisle, so I reminded him to keep them on. I definitely didn't want him to lose them. So I decided that I might as well remind him a second time just to drive home the importance of the message. He agreed and disappeared into one of the aisles. A few minutes later, he dashed out of the aisle with about ten feathered boas around his neck, and happily danced around, being silly. I noticed that he didn't have his glasses on, so I calmly asked, "Where are your glasses, Connor?"

He gasped and said with a smile, "I have no idea!" and continued to act goofy.

I nervously laughed and asked, "Are they in your pocket?"

Still grinning, he rather nonchalantly replied, "No," and proceeded to hippity-hop away.

As calmly as I could, I encouraged Connor to retrace his steps and look for his glasses. He didn't seem to understand the importance of my request, and he wasn't the least bit bothered by having lost them. Connor proceeded to find a small bell to ring, all the while definitely *not* looking for the glasses. I think he thought it was funny and that he was playing an amusing game of sorts, and finding his glasses was the farthest thing from his playful mind. He was having too much fun, and he continued to ignore my instructions. This kind of flippant behavior is honestly my mommy kryptonite.

I could feel my body heat rising. My heart began to beat faster. My cheeks turned red. My voice began to change. And I just know my pupils grew to the size of Junior Mints. It was the kind of metamorphosis you'd expect from Dr. Jekyll as he transitioned into Mr. Hyde. I was morphing into something sinister and crazy. All I could think was, *Why doesn't this kid get it? These are his first and only pair of prescription glasses, and they weren't cheap!* My calm left the building, and I allowed my inner "momster" to take over. With a deep, sharp voice and gnarly face, I commanded Connor to put down his toys and ordered him to start searching for his glasses.

Meanwhile, my then three-year-old, Chandler, escaped from his stroller and ran down one aisle to look at a magnifying glass. I started yelling, "No, Chandler! Come here, right now!" A nice lady who couldn't help but hear my pleas and see my ridiculous predicament tried to help by "keeping an eye out" for the glasses. I am sure my less-than-sincere smile made her doubt my "thankfulness," though I honestly appreciated her kind gesture. I finally got hold of Chandler, just as he opened a bag of candy off the shelf, and I began to put the pressure on Connor once again—all while frantically searching through piles and piles of toys myself.

Just when I thought things couldn't get any worse, they did! I tried explaining to Chandler that the candy he had ripped open wasn't ours, and I took the broken bag from him. For the next ten minutes, he kicked, screamed, and cried, yelling, "My candy!" I had one child acting as if it was funny to lose his glasses, another one screaming and crying about candy that wasn't his, the eldest wandering around aimlessly, and my "baby on board" karate-chopping my abs like he was training for a role in *The Karate Kid*. That was pretty much the riveting climax of our lovely "get-well" shopping experience. Not how I'd envisioned our outing at all. *Sigh.*

It was intense to say the least. We must have been making quite a scene because a Dollar Tree clerk walked up to us and asked, "What is the problem? Can I help?" I told her that Connor had lost his glasses and gave her a description of them. She smiled and offered to search for them as well. In less than a minute, she excitedly said, "Found 'em!" and brought the beloved glasses to me. I slowly turned to Connor, gave him a sinister grin, and demanded that he thank the lady. He nervously smiled and thanked her. Then I leaned over and whispered to him that he was grounded for one week. He didn't say a word.

As we went through the checkout line, I told Connor, once again, to put his glasses on his face. The cashier must have sensed the grit behind my request because she smiled and said, "You better do it, sweetie, or else your mama is gonna spank you right here!" I could feel the eyes of the other customers all over me like daggers. As I stood there, very pregnant with our fourth boy, all I could think about was their likely disapproval of my parenting. I think there might now be a sign in the employee area with our picture and a warning beside it saying something like, BEWARE OF THIS LOONEY TUNES MOTHER AND HER RECKLESS BOYS. Mother of the year right here!

I thanked the clerk once again for her help in finding the glasses, and I hightailed it out of that store. I was so disappointed in Connor—no, I was flabbergasted and enraged by his behavior. More than anything, I was completely embarrassed by my own out-of-control behavior. The last thing I wanted to do was go to our friend's house to deliver a get-well gift. As we walked to the car, Connor found a tree limb—yes, a *limb*—on the median and proceeded to drag it through the parking lot, like a caveman, as if he were going to put it in the van. I sharply said, "Connor, *that* is a tree limb. Put that back on the median and come to the car, *now!*" So what did he decide to do? Throw it, of course, without thinking about how close it was to a car. So I start yelling, "No!" like a crazy person, just as my sweet, mother-of-eight neighbor and her friends walked by. She gave me the most genuine, nonjudgmental smile, and said, "You need another set of hands!" I agreed with that, especially at that moment, I needed another set of hands to get those out-of-control kiddos into my van as fast as possible and then into bed. I was *done*.

When we finally got into the van, frustrated tears poured down my cheeks. I couldn't even speak. I felt like such a failure as a mother *and* as a Christian. I'd allowed my anger—definitely not righteous anger—to get out of control. I'd totally lost my cool. I hadn't exhibited patience or spoken tenderly. My peace was gone.

My eldest son, Cooper, noticed the disappointment all over my face and asked, "Mom, are you crying?"

I didn't want to answer him. I just wanted to go home, put them to bed, and crawl into bed with my husband, but I couldn't. We had planned to do something nice for our friend, and we had to follow through. I had to put my feelings aside and focus on what was most important at that moment. We did that very thing and gave the get-well gift to that sweet little boy. It sure meant a lot to him. We were able to be a blessing, even though our shopping experience was a complete and total bust.

As I've reflected more on that crazy Dollar Tree incident, I have learned a few things:

1. I need to offer more grace and less guilt: They were just a pair of glasses, after all. Yes, Connor needed to be more responsible, but he was learning to wear and care for his brand-new glasses. Children must experience the consequences of their actions, but they need the boundaries to be full of grace, especially when they are learning something new. As Romans 6:14 says, "Sin is no longer your master, for you no longer live under the requirements of the law. Instead, you live under the freedom of God's grace" (NLT).

2. I need to seek forgiveness from God and my children in these kinds of moments: Ultimately, I have an audience of One. But there are little eyes watching my every move as well. I am going to make mistakes, and thank God He offers us so much grace and many chances to get it right. I think it is good for our children to see that we make mistakes and need God's grace, and it is important that we apologize to them when we have blown it as well.

3. I need to be quick to exhibit love and patience: God has lavished His unfailing love on us, and He certainly offers me more patience than I deserve. Why shouldn't I offer my children the same love and patience? Yes, they need clear expectations and consequences for their actions, but I need to be quick to offer them love

and patience instead of judgment and snarky, angry comments. "But you are a God of forgiveness, gracious and merciful, slow to become angry, and rich in unfailing love" (Neh. 9:17 NLT).

4. Chaos is going to happen sometimes, but I don't have to submit to its authority: I have the power to choose panic or peace; it all comes down to who or what I am surrendering to. I want to surrender my heart and home to the Lord every day, but it takes intentionality and consistency on my part. Even so, it is a worthwhile quest that changes the whole climate of my home.

I know this "Dollar Tree Drama" really isn't so terrible in the grand scheme of things. I can now see the silliness behind the whole fiasco. No doubt about it, there *will* be a next time, but I don't have to give way to chaos in the process. I can have and hold on to my peace regardless of the circumstances. I so desperately want peace, patience, love, and kindness to be the consistent climate of our home.

Thankfully, I was able to put my kiddos to bed without anger. We all apologized to each other, and the kids received appropriate consequences. We ended the night by praying together and thanking God for one another and all He is teaching us in our lives—even the hard lessons that can drive us to the plank of chaos.

Maybe you are right at the edge of the plank today, Sweet Mama. You are exhausted, frustrated, and forlorn. You feel like you have no other choice than to jump into the choppy waters of chaos. You don't know how to get your peace back, or if you've ever really experienced God's peace before. Friend, you don't have to give way to the pressures, accusations, and shame that the enemy tries to place on you through chaos. Get. Off. That. Plank. Take a breath. A deep one. Say a prayer that God will give you the patience and peace you need to be the mom He's called you to be— a loving, caring, hardworking, devoted, humble, fun, and completely imperfect mother who refuses to give up and surrender to the peace pirates—even on those days when you feel like you are walking the plank.

Life, as beautiful and amazing as it is, can be exhausting. In an effort to stay ahead, or simply keep up, we push and push and push ourselves to achieve. And then sometimes, the only thing we have to show for it is our worn-out, shell-like self, crying out for stillness.

Peace. We need peace in our lives, or we won't experience the full life that God so desires us to possess. We are designed to have His peace in our lives. But how do we find it? Peace comes from God, and it is a blessing and a gift that we receive with His Holy Spirit. Psalm 29:11 says, "The LORD gives strength to his people; the LORD blesses his people with peace." I love how the psalmist lists "strength" and "peace" in the same sentence, and I believe that is on purpose. It is hard to be strong without also having peace. If we are married, we must have peace in our marriage to have a strong marriage. We may have tense moments of disagreement or crazy schedules in different seasons of our marriage and family, but throughout it all, we must find peace. As mothers, we must have peace in our relationship with our kids or we will not cultivate a strong bond with our children. This doesn't mean that there is an absence of chaos or friction. We can't always control our circumstances. God's peace as defined in the Bible comes from the Hebrew word *shalom*. Isn't that such a beautiful word? Like most Hebrew words, *shalom* has a deeper meaning than one English word can describe. The literal translation of *shalom* would be "completeness." According to John A. Benner's ancient-hebrew.org, referring to *Strong's Hebrew Dictionary of the Bible* (#7965), *shalom* is "Something that has been finished or made whole. A state of being complete." Wow! Isn't that so beautiful? So when we read the Bible verses about peace with the knowledge of this deeper meaning, we can interchange the word "peace" with the words "completeness" and "wholeness." Let's try it with Psalm 29:11: "The LORD gives strength to his people; the LORD blesses his people with wholeness."

Strength and wholeness. God willingly offers us both of these amazing gifts just because He loves us and wants us to walk boldly under His authority. Strong and courageous. Lacking nothing. Complete because He makes us complete. Strong because He gives us strength. Ready to face anything.

This kind of peace comes in the form of knowing we will get through the hard times and come out the other side. It is an assurance that God is with us and for us. However, it is not an easy pursuit. Some days, it's really hard to find peace—to feel complete—in the craziness of family life, especially in the child-rearing and career-building years. The enemy wants to throw us off our game. He'd love nothing more than to make us feel like we are ill-equipped for the task of motherhood. He'd love to bust up our marriages, cause our kids to disconnect from us, and make us so busy with work, school, church, and other obligations that we don't even see the peace pirates plundering our hearts and homes. That's the enemy's game. Always has been. But we don't have to live in fear or throw up a white flag of surrender. We just have to stay alert and make sure that God is at the helm of our mothership. He is our captain who will lovingly guide us to where we need to go. Even so, it's not going to happen without a fight.

As I was studying the meaning of *shalom* in *Strong's Hebrew*, I noticed another Hebrew word that was eerily close in pronunciation, yet drastically different in meaning. I saw the word *shalal*. As I further investigated the meaning of this word, I couldn't believe what I found. *Shalal* is "Plunder taken from an enemy in war or robbery. To impair the quality or effect of." The English word they assigned to *shalal* was "spoil." Some additional meanings of *shalal* are "plunder, destroy, prey." My heart literally skipped a beat as I read this, and when I discovered the ancient Hebrew word pictures for *shalom* and *shalal*, my understanding of God's peace was forever changed. Here are the ancient Hebrew word pictures for each:

shalom

shalal

They share a couple of the same word pictures. Here is what each picture stands for:

water, chaos

shepherd's staff, authority

tent peg, to attach

strong teeth, to destroy

The ancient Hebrew word pictures illustrate the meaning of *shalom* as "to destroy the authority attached to chaos," and *shalal* as "to gain authority through de-struction." How fitting are these descriptions? These depictions reiterate the truth that peace is a gift from God, but it is not one that we can keep without a fight. We are at war with the master of destruction trying to eat away at our peace—with distractions, busyness, frustration, and exhaustion. When we surrender to chaos and put ourselves under its authority, we will lose a piece of ourselves every time. Our sanity. Our self-worth. Our faith. *Our peace.*

Thank God, we don't have to give way to the thieves that want to plunder the peace God has given us and be ruled by chaos and destruction. We have a God who wants us to live a life where we are complete and whole in Him. He is our shepherd who gently but efficiently takes His shepherd crook to our necks and pulls us out of the grip of chaos and destruction and into His presence—under His tender, loving, healing care. He lifts our head and holds us tight, and He alone restores what chaos and destruction stole from us. He makes us whole again, and we experience His perfect peace.

When I read Scripture through the lens of this knowledge of the extended definition of peace as taken from the original Hebrew, I stand in awe. Peace—*shalom*—is consistently addressed and seen as something worth protecting, pursuing, and promoting in our lives. I think about David writing Psalm 23, in which he describes a detailed and beautiful picture of being at peace with the Lord, even in the midst of chaos around him:

The LORD is my shepherd, **I lack nothing**.
He makes me lie down in green pastures,
he leads me beside **quiet waters**,
he refreshes my soul.
He guides me along the right paths
for his name's sake.
Even though I walk
through the darkest valley,
I will fear no evil,
for you are with me;
your rod and your staff,
they comfort me.
You prepare a table before me
in the presence of my enemies.
You anoint my head with oil;
my cup overflows.
Surely your goodness and love will follow me
all the days of my life,
and I will dwell in the house of the LORD
forever.

I emphasized certain lines to point out how much David's eloquent words line up with the Bible's definition of *shalom*. To "lack nothing" is one of the literal meanings of *shalom*. David was proclaiming that He had peace. "Quiet waters" are the opposite of the ancient Hebrew word picture that depicts choppy waters as representing chaos. Isn't that so cool? God always brings order out of chaos. "Even though I walk through the darkest valley," I don't have to allow my fear to give way to chaos when

I am in God's presence. Isn't that the best news for those of us who feel like our peace is waning on a daily basis? Friend, we don't have to walk that plank. A plank is a place of shame. It's isolating and accusing. It has a width that supports only one person, but God never wants us to go through life feeling ashamed, unsteady, and alone. He wants us to face every day with Him and under His loving care and authority. That is the only way we can pursue, protect, and promote His perfect peace in our lives.

But how do we practically do that? First of all, we must realize that God's peace is *given*, not achieved. Psalm 122:7–8 says, "May there be peace within your walls and security within your citadels. For the sake of my family and friends, I will say, 'Peace be within you.'"

I love how it says, "within your walls." Here, the psalmist is offering a prayer of peace over Jerusalem, and the first place he asks for peace is inside their homes. Next, he asks for the "citadels," or places of governing, to be secure. Verse 8, however, is more personal in nature. It's more about relationships. In other words, the psalmist is saying, for the sake of those whom I love the most, I hope that you have God's peace in your heart because that one thing affects *everything*. Our decisions. How we treat others. How we deal with conflict and accomplishments. If we don't have God's peace within our hearts, then we are lacking what we need to be at our best for God, ourselves, and others. We are ill-equipped and much more susceptible to surrendering to the authority of chaos. Losing our temper. Making the wrong choices. Misplacing our priorities. Neglecting our relationship with the Lord and our loved ones.

This is something I have struggled with over the years, especially since I've become a mother. I *love* being a mom. It is one of the greatest blessings of my life. But if I'm honest, motherhood has been hard on my marriage at times. Over the years, I've found that I'm not the only married mom who feels this way.

Last year, I put out a call on social media asking moms about some of the hurdles they face when it comes to being both a wife *and* a mom. Some of you may have filled out this mom questionnaire that I issued via e-mail (thank you!). Time after time, those surveyed said that striving to balance marriage and motherhood is one of their biggest struggles. There is so much guilt, resentment, pride, and disappointment around this issue, and sometimes it feels like our pursuit to "succeed" in motherhood is literally killing our marriage, not to mention the peace in our heart and home.

Here's what one mom had to say:

> "Both of my children are under five and require a tremendous amount of attention and energy—for keeping up with, training, supervising, and general care. Everything is new and unexpected. It is difficult to attend to other areas at the same time, such as cleaning and maintaining my home, work/projects/other commitments outside of home, and marriage."
>
> —Stephanie M., married with two kids

Our kids are always on our minds, and they should be. We're reading parenting books, looking into the best schools and colleges, and making sure they are healthy and well-rounded individuals. We're attending their activities and going to parent-teacher conferences. We're talking with other moms about our kiddos to make sure we are on the right track and in the know. We're up at night praying that God will protect our children, heal our children, and help our children become the individuals He made them to be. We're shedding tears over the fact that we lost our temper that day and said things we didn't mean. We pray that God will help us to be better tomorrow, and sometimes, it is better. Sometimes it's not, and we feel frustrated and defeated. In our lowest and most exhausted moments, we wonder if we even have what it takes to be a "good" mom and wife at the same time. Some days, we're not sure if it is even possible to succeed at both. If we're honest, we're not sure what succeeding at both even looks like. Is it having high-achieving kids and not getting divorced in the process of raising those kids? Is it raising children in a home where nobody ever has an argument? Is it getting to the end of the child-rearing years and having grown kids and a spouse who you actually like being around? What is *it*?

Friend, being the best mom and wife we can be is a worthwhile quest, and we should certainly strive to be our best. However, we can't be at our best without God's peace in our heart. It's hard to be a loving spouse and parent when your heart isn't whole, and some of us need to stop expecting our spouse and children to fill the gaps in our hearts. Though our spouse and family are certainly always in our heart, they were never meant to make us whole. They don't have that capability. Our spouse and children are gifts from God, but they are also flawed human beings—just like us. They're going to let us down. They're going to make us crazy at times. They're going to bring us joy and pain and everything in between. They are what makes our lives richer and sweeter, but we can't expect them to make us whole. Only God can do that. Only God can bring us *shalom*. And when we focus on getting off the plank and running back to His embrace, He will make us whole again and again and again. Thank You, Jesus!

So, Married Mamas, can we be a good wife *and* a good mom at the same time? Absolutely. This will happen naturally when we put God first by fostering our relationship with Him and pursuing His peace in our lives, continue to prioritize and invest in our marriage, and then work *together* to train our children up in the way they should go (Prov. 22:6 ESV) through the highs and lows of life.

Peace is at the heart of every healthy relationship, and I would even venture to say that peace is priceless. It is one of the greatest blessings that God has freely given us, and yet most of us struggle to find it and keep it. I love how Solomon, known as being one of the wisest men in history, describes God's peace in Proverbs 17:1. He writes, "Better a dry crust eaten in peace than a house filled with feasting— and conflict" (NLT). If Solomon were living in this day and age, he could declare that one pointed statement at a church service or Ted Talk and drop the mic right after. Seriously, though. Isn't what he wrote so true?

Wouldn't you rather have a peaceful home and peace-filled heart than a Thanksgiving-style feast with all the fixin's along with a dollop of cynicism and family angst sprinkled on top? I would choose peace every single time, but unfortunately, I don't. Why is that? Because I am often blind to my own desperate need for it until the damage is done. I've flown off the handle at my kids. I've ignored emotional cues from my husband. I've neglected my quiet time with the Lord. I run, run, run, and do "all the things" while ignoring the very thing that keeps me grounded, levelheaded, full-hearted, and at my best. So "all the things" end up running me ragged and render me exhausted and frustrated at my loved ones and my circumstances. Chaos ends up getting my allegiance on those days, and I go to sleep seeking God's forgiveness while feeling like a failure.

Can you relate, Sweet Mama? I bet you can, or you wouldn't have opened this book in the first place. You long for God's peace as much as I do. I want you to know that you can have it. We don't have to constantly feel like we are somehow missing the mark as a mother. We don't have to give way to chaos and allow it to rule our lives regardless of how many kids we have, or the level of financial hardship we are facing, or the marital difficulty we are having, or how exhausted we are from *all the things*! We can't always prevent chaos, but we *can* keep it from stealing our joy and peace in the process. Friend, we do this by making it our mission to pursue God's peace *every single day* whether we feel like it or not. We so desperately need it, and God so clearly wants us to have it.

In Psalm 34:14, the psalmist writes, "Turn from evil and

do good; seek peace and pursue it." Peace isn't just going to find us; we have to seek and pursue it *every day*. But how do we do this, especially with everything else we are desperately trying to do?

As I write this, I am staring at the mounds—seriously, mounds—of laundry on my washer and dryer that have yet to be put away after weeks of travel. I need to fill out school forms, go to the grocery, call my sweet friends whom I haven't talked to in quite a while, write thank-you notes, and I would love to plan a weekend away with my hot hubby sans kids, but things have been so *ca-ray-zee* lately that I come to the end of the day just wanting—no, craving—a moment of solitude. Stillness. Peace.

I used to feel a bit guilty about this. I mean, why can't I just pour into everybody and everything else and be okay? At times, I've even accepted the lie that I simply don't have enough time to pursue peace each day. However, the more I've thought and prayed about this, the more I've come to realize that God doesn't want me to live a life without peace and stillness. God is the author and provider of peace. He desires for all of us to have peace that can come only from Him and be experienced in relationship with Him, every single day of our lives. Yet on so many days, we metaphorically walk the plank and allow the chaos to overtake us, and we are left feeling defeated and depleted. Lacking. Less than whole. Experiencing more *shalal* in our lives than *shalom*. So how do we resist this negative cycle? Psalm 46:10 says, "Be still, and know that I am God."

When you feel like everything is falling apart and you don't know what to do:

Be still and know . . .

When you are burned out and you feel like you have nothing good left to give your family at the end of a hectic day:

Be still and know . . .

When you have worked so hard to create the life around you and suddenly things just don't seem to be going in your favor:

Be still and know . . .

When we consciously choose to take a moment in our day to be quiet and pray for God to help us have His peace in our lives, He promises to give it to us. It may not come the way we expect it to, but He will provide it. We must choose to be still and know that He is God. God will never fail us. Philippians 4:7, one of my favorite verses, states so well what His peace provides: "And the peace of God, which transcends all understanding, will guard your hearts and your minds in Christ Jesus."

The author, Paul, points out that God's peace is so great and mysterious that it is beyond human comprehension. Not only that, but it protects our hearts and minds. That is precisely why we desperately need it. Life is full of twists and turns, and it seems like the busier my schedule gets, the less peace I feel within myself and at home. I don't want it to be that way. If we are too busy to pursue peace through a quiet moment of stillness and prayer, then we are *too* busy, period. Sweet Mama, I am talking to myself here, and I am hearing it loud and clear. We will keep on marching down that plank and surrendering to chaos unless we become very intentional about pursuing, promoting, and protecting His peace in our hearts and homes.

A huge factor in carrying out this quest is recognizing what is trying to steal our peace—the *peace pirates*. In these next four chapters, we are going to explore the four peace pirates that are chipping away at our hearts and ransacking our homes: *mommy martyrdom, comparison chaos, clenching control,* and *excessive expectations*. You will learn how to identify your primary peace pirate and how you can guard yourself from its tricky tactics.

We are all affected by each of the peace pirates to some degree, but some hit our hearts and homes harder than others. The key to fighting these peace pirates is to realize that we are engaging in spiritual warfare each and every day. John 10:10–18 makes this clear in sharing Jesus' words to His disciples, where he refers to Satan (our enemy) as "the thief." He states:

> The thief comes only to steal and kill and destroy; I have come that they may have life, and have it to the full.
>
> I am the good shepherd. The good shepherd lays down his life for the sheep. The hired hand is not the shepherd and does not own the sheep. So when he sees the wolf coming, he abandons the sheep and runs away. Then the wolf attacks the flock and scatters it. The man runs away because he is a hired hand and cares nothing for the sheep.
>
> I am the good shepherd; I know my sheep and my sheep know me—just as the Father knows me and

I know the Father—and I lay down my life for the sheep. I have other sheep that are not of this sheep pen. I must bring them also. They too will listen to my voice, and there shall be one flock and one shepherd. The reason my Father loves me is that I lay down my life—only to take it up again. No one takes it from me, but I lay it down of my own accord. I have authority to lay it down and authority to take it up again. This command I received from my Father.

Once again, the Lord uses the metaphor of a shepherd and his flock to depict how He leads us and takes great care of us. He illustrates the great divide between Him—the Shepherd—and Satan (the enemy)—"the thief," "the hired hand," and "the wolf." I find it so interesting that just like the Holy Trinity—God the Father, Jesus the Son, and the Holy Spirit—Jesus describes the enemy as having three representations with one unholy, sinister, and ultimately careless mission. The thief's aim is to steal, kill, and destroy us. The hired hand abandons the sheep when they need him the most, and he runs away as the wolf attacks the flock and causes them to scatter. We can only assume that in a situation like this one, many of the sheep would be killed, others would be injured, and the rest would be running for their lives wondering why the hired hand didn't protect them. Thank God, it doesn't have to be this way! Jesus continues his beautiful word picture, a parable, by declaring that He would never lead His sheep, or in other words His followers—His beloved kids—in this destructive, manipulative, and careless way. He calls Himself "the good shepherd." I love that. He stresses that because He is the good shepherd, He knows, cares for, and leads His sheep. And they—we—know Him. Jesus even makes it crystal clear that He alone is the *shepherd*, taking away the confusion or chaos that only a thief, hired hand, or wolf would bring the sheep.

In this parable, Jesus also points out that the hired hand "does not own the sheep" and "cares nothing for the sheep." In other words, the hired hand just wanted to control the sheep for a time and for his own gain. The hired hand never intended to take responsibility for the sheep and protect them. In the same way, a thief's only prerogative is to get what he wants by any means necessary, and he cares nothing about the person he steals from. A wolf is ruled by his own ferocious animal instincts to kill and feast on his prey, and he cares nothing about the lives that he takes.

Friend, do you see the common theme here? Our enemy, Satan, wants only to control us for his own gain. Under his authority, there is no peace. Instead we get confusion, heartache, emptiness, and fear. On the other hand, "God is not a God of disorder but of peace..." (1 Cor.14:33). Sweet Mama, don't you take comfort in this truth? I sure do. We have a God who loves us, protects us, and makes us whole. Even when we find ourselves caught under the authority of chaos and destruction—the thief, the hired hand, the wolf, the enemy—our good shepherd takes his staff and gently pulls us back into His safe and loving care. He finds every lost sheep that was scattered by the wolf, brings them home, and rejoices (Luke 15:1–7). His heart breaks when he sees his sheep hurting, and he weeps when they are overtaken (John 11:35). He brings life to the otherwise dead (Luke 8:54–55), and He restores what has been stolen from us (Joel 2:25).

He truly is our good shepherd, who will lead you and help you to pursue, promote, and protect His peace in your heart and home.

A prayer for the mama who feels like she is walking the plank:

Dear Lord,

Thank You for loving us the way You do. I surrender my life and my family to You, Lord. I am tired and weary from the chaos and destruction the enemy is wreaking in my life. I long for Your peace. I want to step off this plank and into Your loving arms. I need You, Lord. I am Yours.

In Jesus' name,
Amen

PART II

The Four Peace Pirates

CHAPTER FOUR

Mommy Martyrdom

Key Principle: Failing to take time to care for ourselves limits our ability to adequately and lovingly care for others.

"By the time I have finished everything I could accomplish in a day, I sit down and realize all the things I should have or could have accomplished. So then, I'm not only exhausted, but I'm feeling guilty and like a slacker for not doing 478,393 more things that day."

—Miki W., married mom of three

Have you ever had one of those mornings when you feel like you are running around like the Energizer Bunny—going and going and going—but not quite keeping up with everything and everyone? I sure have. I'm not exactly a morning person, but honestly, I so wish that I were. Life would be so much easier for my family and me. Or at least I think it would. I'm more of a night person. My mind just won't shut off until around 11:30 p.m., and with a good hour's worth of *Law & Order: SVU*. Seriously, what is it about Detectives Stabler and Benson that lulls me to sleep? Am I the only one, or am I a total weirdo? Either way, it's my routine.

So when 6:30 a.m. rolls around, I'm not exactly raring to go, but I have to muster up my best energy and face the day. However, I don't necessarily get the time I need to "muster." I usually wake up to a four-year-old rolling over and elbowing me in the face. He crawls into our bed every day in the wee hours of the morning to cuddle. It's so sweet. Honestly, I'm eating it up because he's our baby, but it is not the best way to wake up—especially for a non-morning person. After my elbow alarm clock goes off, I roll out of bed and feel my way to the kitchen. My first quest is coffee. Oh, how I love the dark black liquid pick-me-up. This, friends, is my means to "muster." My husband and kids know how I am wired, and they sweetly and patiently respect my ten-minute coffee time. Now, don't get me wrong. It's not a quiet coffee time. It usually consists of me sitting beside my three non-morning kids who are in blanket cocoons on the couch watching cartoons for a few minutes while my one morning-loving son is almost skipping laps around the kitchen, ready to face the day. He, along with my amazing husband, Dave, are talking and buzzing about. Meanwhile, the other kids and I are still mustering together.

After those ten minutes, we realize that whatever energy

we've mustered up has got to be enough to face the day, and so we consciously choose to face it—often hesitantly and even begrudgingly at times. *Sigh*. Then it's off to the races to get our four kids ready and off to their four different schools. We make sure backpacks are packed correctly with water bottles, snacks, and lunches. Side note—does anyone else find it interesting that every school seems to require a water bottle and snack for kids each day? What happened to just eating lunch (and sometimes breakfast) at school and coming home starving and scarfing down a snack? No big deal, but my goodness, our kids sure have it good these days and they don't even know it. Anyway, after we pack accordingly, we make sure mouths are wiped, shoes are on, our bus riders are off, and our car riders are buckled into their seats correctly. Then I look down at my bare feet and realize that in the midst of getting everyone else ready, I've forgotten that I'm still in my pajamas—which usually consist of yoga pants, a T-shirt, and sometimes a robe. So, I rush back to my room, put on something more presentable, throw on some shoes, run back to the minivan, and head to the school drop-off line.

One morning, I was running especially late, but I was determined to make it to the drop-off line on time. I knew something had to give, so I got the kids dressed, packed, and ready, and jumped into the driver's seat with a pink fleece robe on, pajamas underneath, and Christmas reindeer house shoes. Also, I had slight bedhead, which I tried to form into a sort of messy bun (which is supposedly in these days, so there's that), and no makeup on. I hoped and prayed I wouldn't see any of my neighbors, and God forbid I would get pulled over or have to physically get my first-grader out of the car.

I entered the drop-off line and hunkered down, hoping that I wouldn't make eye contact with any of the other parent drivers or teachers helping with the line. I had to come to a full stop—of course—so I tried to adjust the top of my robe to make it look more like a jacket and less "robe-ish," and pressed the button to let Chandler out of the van. When the teacher came up to assist, I said hello to her and good-bye to Chandler with a nervous side glance and half smile, and exited the zone as quickly as I could. The friendly gym teacher saw me and waved, with a confused expression on his face. I waved back quickly and kept on going.

As I made my way back home, I thought to myself, *Why am I feeling so nervous about this? I am totally winning right now!* I surprised myself with this line of thinking, but the more I let those thoughts sink in, the better I felt. Why had I been putting so much pressure on myself to look a certain way to drop off my first-grader when I didn't even have to exit the car? So I decided to get ready when I got home—in the quiet. It was amazing. I knew this wasn't something that I would do every morning, but it was definitely something I would do every now and then to relieve some of the morning pressure. Mornings are nuts, so not having to get myself ready in a breakneck fashion brought me more peace and perspective.

I was so excited about this shift in my morning routine and new personal revelation that I decided to snap a pic of my outfit and share what I'd learned on Facebook. So many mothers responded with comments of solidarity and humor, yet others were more critical. One mom said, "I would never do this! If I expect my kids to get fully dressed and ready in the morning before school, then I need to set a good example and do the same."

Honestly, I get the point. We certainly need to set a good example for our children whenever we can. However, I believe this sweet mama didn't understand the heart behind my post. As mothers, we carry so much weight on our shoulders. We strive to meet our children's needs and teach them how to be good citizens. As Christian mothers, we try to show them Jesus. If we are married, we strive to show our children what a healthy and loving marriage looks like, and in an effort to do that, we try to invest in our relationship with our husband and do our best to tend to his needs as well. As daughters, we lovingly care for our aging parents and try to attend to their changing needs. As sisters, we touch base with our siblings and try to keep a close relationship. As friends, we foster our friendships by being available when our friends need us the most. As coworkers, we aim to be punctual, persistent, and professional in our working relationships. I could go on, but the list would consume this entire chapter. Bottom line, we all wear many different hats and are striving to meet all kinds of different needs. And it can wear us down.

It's a wonderful blessing to have so many people in our life whom we love and who love us, but it can also be a heavy burden to bear—especially in the thick of motherhood. It can take nearly all of our time and energy to the point where we can lose our center, and desperately need to recalibrate. Many of us live off-kilter for years without even realizing that we are approaching life and our loved ones in a lopsided, misguided fashion. It's during this season of mounting pressure, constant decision making, lack of sleep, and little downtime that a particularly pesky peace pirate tries to wiggle its way into our hearts and homes. I like to call this one "Mommy Martyrdom." It's a stealthy one because it seems so harmless on the surface. When I think of the word "martyr," my first thought goes right to the Christian martyrs who lost their lives for refusing to renounce their belief in Jesus. We hold them in high esteem in the church and throughout history, and we absolutely should.

However, there is another kind of "martyrdom" that is not about drawing attention to the Lord but bringing attention to ourselves. It's a "look at how much *I* have given up" attitude. It's a "see how much *I* do for everyone else compared to the very little *I* do for myself" kind of approach. These stances don't seem inherently bad on the surface, do they? Sacrifice is certainly part of loving someone, and it's good to do more for others than yourself, right? Of course! But when our primary motivation for doing these things is to make others think more highly of us or to make ourselves feel good about ourselves, then we are missing it. That's not love, friend. That's just pride, insecurity, and a lack of trust in God. And those three things poke enormous holes in the fortress of peace around our heart and home, and make us extremely vulnerable to the Mommy Martyrdom peace pirate.

So how can we tell if Mommy Martyrdom is pillaging

our heart and home? A good place to start is looking at our priorities. When we make decisions, are our children our very first thought every single time? Do we schedule our lives around them? Do we see it as our duty to satisfy their every need? Do we spend so much time with them that we rarely, if ever, have time to invest in our marriage? Do we forgo quiet time, sleep, exercise, coffee with a friend, and things we might enjoy in order to do things for our children? If "yes" is the answer to any of these questions, then you might be struggling with Mommy Martyrdom. It does seem honorable on the surface, but it's completely out of balance when we take a deeper look.

When you look up the word "martyr," it's defined as "voluntarily suffering death for something someone believes in." Christian martyrdom is honorable because those people—not actively pursuing death—were threatened with death for their beliefs unless they renounced those beliefs. Yet despite facing death, they chose to proclaim the name of Jesus. These martyrs knew that death was not the end for those who follow Jesus; they chose to be strong and courageous even in the midst of being slain, burned at the stake, or hung on an upside-down cross. They chose to worship God to the end rather than being prevented from worshipping Him or having a relationship with Him. Martyrdom is a tragedy because people's lives were unjustly ended too soon. But it's also something God honors because they died for the object of their worship: Him, the King of Kings.

The key takeaway here is that God may allow some to be martyrs for His glory to increase the faith of others. But

He never calls us to be martyrs for our children or family, because they were not created to be the object of our worship. They aren't supposed to be our center. God alone is. In Matthew 6:30–33, Jesus says, "But seek first his kingdom and his righteousness..." As Christ's followers, God must be our first thought, the sole object of worship, and our primary guide. I love how *The Message* further explains this verse:

> If God gives such attention to the appearance of wildflowers—most of which are never even seen—don't you think he'll attend to you, take pride in you, do his best for you? What I'm trying to do here is to get you to relax, to not be so preoccupied with *getting*, so you can respond to God's *giving*. People who don't know God and the way he works fuss over these things, but you know both God and how he works. Steep your life in God-reality, God-initiative, God-provisions. Don't worry about missing out. You'll find all your everyday human concerns will be met.

Man, that verse hits me right between the eyes. When we've fallen prey to Mommy Martyrdom, we believe the lie that we need to work ourselves to the bone to prove that we are a "good" mom. We feel like we need to get our kids from activity to activity while eating fast food on the run and wearing ourselves out to give them the best opportunities. We think we need to be on every school committee and make school crafts until the middle of the night to prove that we are investing in their education. We

try to throw the very best Pinterest-perfect birthday parties with the very best party favors and food to show our
kids we love them. We stretch our budgets thin to dress
our kids in the very best clothes so that they (and we) are
perceived as being "well-to-do." We feel the need to practically do school projects for our children so they get high
marks and look good to the teacher.

All the while, we neglect ourselves. We rarely if ever get
the sleep our body needs. Our body aches for rest, and
our mind is desperate for reprieve. But we ignore it and
press on through. We wake up and hit the ground running
without giving a single thought to what we might need to
be at our best. We feel guilty getting ourselves that new
shirt we've had our eye on at Target because we could get
our kids a new shirt instead. We keep denying ourselves.
We always feel like we are playing catch-up. We never feel
rested, but we tell ourselves it's okay because it's "for the
kids." We rarely have a date night with our spouse because
we believe we must spend that date night money "on the
kids" instead. And we wonder why we feel disconnected
from our spouse. We don't like the body we see in the mirror or how we feel when we wake up, but we tell ourselves
that it's just how it has to be because we don't have the
time or energy after doing everything we have to do "for
the kids." We put on a smile, but many days we feel like
crying or maybe screaming into a pillow, and instead, we
usually end up snapping at our spouse and children. We are
wearing thin by the day, and we constantly feel insecure
about ourselves and our family. We tell ourselves that our
lives are supposed to revolve around our kids in this par-

enting season and that sacrificing our own sanity and even our health is par for the course. But deep in our hearts, we *ache* for God's peace.

Sound familiar, Sweet Mama? I've honestly been there more than I'd like to admit. There were years when I neglected my self-care "for my kids," and it only led to me gaining thirty pounds, harboring resentment toward my husband and kids, perpetually lashing out at my family, and nearly having a total mental and emotional breakdown. The more we allow the Mommy Martyrdom peace pirate to wreak havoc in our lives, the more prone we are to having mental and emotional health issues. Our mental and emotional health is extremely important, and it affects everything and everyone in our lives. We can't take proper care of ourselves or anyone else when we are struggling mentally and emotionally.

According to the Anxiety and Depression Association of America, "Anxiety disorders are the most common mental illness in the United States, affecting 40 million adults age 18 and older, or 18.1% of the population." It also states that "Anxiety disorders are highly treatable, yet only about 36.9% of those suffering receive treatment." When left untreated, they can take a tremendous toll on one's family.

In my early twenties, I started experiencing depression and anxiety firsthand, but I didn't realize it at the time. That's the funny thing about these disorders. We think it's *normal* at first, because we assume it will pass on its own. Human beings are prone to having some anxious thoughts. We tell ourselves things like, "I'm just *worried*. I'll snap out of it in time." Or, "I'm just *down*. I'll get better when my circumstances get better." Or, "I'm just *a little nervous*. It will pass."

All people have these thoughts a time or two, but those suffering with anxiety and depression let these "every now and then" thoughts turn into habitual and accusing thoughts. They fester and become more sinister by the day, and those who suffer do so in silence and shame. Over time, those of us with anxiety and depression start thinking and *believing* thoughts like, "I will never snap out of this. I must have done something terribly wrong to feel this way." Or, "I'm going to *lose* everything and completely *mess up* my family." Or, "If anyone knew the worries and horrible thoughts I have, they would reject me. I can't tell anyone about this."

Friend, if any of these thoughts sound familiar, then you know the pain of living with anxiety and depression. You have what some refer to as "functional" anxiety and depression if you live with the weight of this every single day but you are still able to complete your basic responsibilities as a spouse, a parent, a worker, etc. However, you feel like your mind, heart, and body are daily being sucker-punched as you are riddled with accusing thoughts, a churning stomach, and heavy breathing. You may even experience intense anxiety attacks, too. You feel like you can't tell anyone because you don't understand what brought this on, and you don't expect anyone else to either.

Friend, I'm here to tell you that *you are not alone*. You did not do anything to bring this on, and most important, you can get the help you need. In fact, *you must!* I tell you this as someone who walked through a long, four-year battle with anxiety and depression. I know how hard it is on a marriage and kids. I understand how it feels to wake up in the middle of the night in a cold sweat, having a full-blown anxiety attack, and running to the bathroom to throw up. I know the overwhelming fear of losing your spouse and the frustration of not being able to just "snap out of it." It's gut-wrenching and heartbreaking, but *there is hope.*

Oh, friend, if you are dealing with this, my heart breaks for you and with you, but please believe me when I tell you that you absolutely can be free from this! There is hope when we open up to our spouse and trusted family and friends about our struggle. We cannot keep it in. The only way we can get help is by being honest and open. Hope is not hiding in the dark; it can *only* be found in the light because it is a gift from the Lord. So we must be brave and bring this truth to light by sharing our deepest fears, worries, and anxieties first and foremost with the Lord, and then, with those we love most.

As Christian mothers, we often shy away from talking about our mental health battles because we think we are the only ones who have deep and dark doubts, fears, and anxieties. We tell ourselves that we must be "crazy" or "damaged." That is a lie from the enemy. It's one of his best tactics that he uses to throw us off our path and into a prison of shame. Friend, God loves you and He knows your every thought. It doesn't scare Him or even make Him turn away from you. It breaks His heart to see you hurting, tossing and turning, crying, and feeling ashamed. He so desperately wants to bring You His perfect peace. He is right there with you. You just have to surrender your fears, your worries, your doubts, your pride, your insecurity—your every thought—to Him.

In my own experience, I wouldn't have survived my four-year battle with anxiety and depression without the full support of my husband. There were times I would wake him up in the middle of the night to ask for prayer and an encouraging word. He lovingly prayed for me and encouraged me every single time. I truly believe that God heard our prayers and strengthened both of us through that difficult time. Prayer has been and continues to be my lifeline of hope. Dave also encouraged me to attend Christian counseling. My counselors were a tremendous help to me, and I attended counseling on a weekly basis. Each session, my counselors would help me unpack the root of my depression and anxiety, give me practical tools to help with my healing, and remind me of the truth in God's Word. I felt lighter and lighter with every appointment. Today, I am living in freedom, and I am quick to tell anyone suffering with depression and anxiety that *you can live in freedom, too!* Your battle with anxiety and depression doesn't define your life, so please don't believe those lies that the enemy is telling you.

Friends, we are engaged in spiritual warfare, and mental and emotional health issues are one way that the enemy tries to poke holes in our peace. He tries to convince us that we are to blame for those holes he made, and when we choose to believe him, we run and hide in shame.

Every battle requires a fight, so we must keep on fighting *against* the anxiety and depression by resisting the desire to hide our struggle. Bring those lies in your mind to the light, and surrender them to God. Lay them at His feet. He will cover you in His truth and show you that you are not damaged goods. He will mend your broken heart (Ps. 147:3) and renew your mind (Rom. 12:2). He will bring you peace.

God's Word says that we are "fearfully and wonderfully made" (Ps. 139:14). The New Living Translation rephrases this as "wonderfully complex." Don't you just love that? We are complex creatures whom God designed for a great purpose. It's crystal clear in His Word that He doesn't want us to be anxious. Philippians 4:6–7 says, "Do not be anxious about anything, but in every situation, by prayer and petition, with thanksgiving, present your requests to God. And the peace of God, which transcends all understanding, will guard your hearts and your minds in Christ Jesus." In John 14:27, Jesus tells us, "Peace I leave with you; my peace I give you. I do not give to you as the world gives. Do not let your hearts be troubled and do not be afraid."

Anxiety and depression are not easy battles to face, and we certainly can't face them alone. If you are struggling with this, please open up to your spouse, trusted family member, or close friend. Find a local Christian counselor or pastor to talk to on a regular basis. Tell your doctor, too. In certain situations, antidepressants or anti-anxiety medication may be helpful.

You do not have to keep on suffering with this, and you *will* get through it. There will come a day when you *will* walk in freedom. It may take some time—more time than you realize right now—but I promise you that freedom will come when you refuse to give up and continue to get the help you need.

Let today be your first step to freedom!

The truth is that your mental and emotional health correlates directly to your spiritual health. And when you are wrestling with Mommy Martyrdom, your spiritual health suffers greatly. You won't be able to stay under God's authority and keep your peace when you neglect your relationship with Him. Yes, He loves us no matter what and is there for us through everything, but *we* are rejecting His specialized spiritual training and weapons that you seriously need to fend off the plunderers of our peace.

We train our minds and hearts to develop a kind of spiritual insight, focus, and strategy every time we open the Bible and study His Word. The more we read God's Word and pray, the more we grow in our relationship with Him and recalibrate our mind, heart, and life to trust God as the center and guiding force of our perspective and approach to everything and everyone. I love how the prophet Isaiah describes this in Isaiah 26:3: "You [God] will keep in perfect peace those whose minds are steadfast, because they trust in you." I find those words so comforting but also very refining. Dictionary.com defines "steadfast" as unwavering, fixed, and resolute. According to Isaiah 26:3, the pathway to steadfastness starts with trusting the Lord.

Trust. It seems so simple, yet you and I both know that it's much easier said than done—especially when it comes to our kids. Yet we can't find and keep His peace and keep the peace pirates at bay unless we put our trust in Him. When we trust the Lord, we are placing ourselves in His loving care and under His authority, which means chaos will not overwhelm us. This doesn't mean it won't exist. It just means that every day we have a choice. Are we going to place ourselves under the authority of chaos by surrendering to the Mommy Martyrdom peace pirates, or are we going to surrender our heart and home to the Lord and stay under His authority, which yields peace regardless of our circumstances? Please consciously choose the latter, friend.

Some of you may be reading this and thinking, *I don't currently struggle with mental or emotional health issues, but I just can't seem to find the time to take care of myself. If only I could just have a break!* I feel you, Mama. Being a mom often means taking care of everyone else *except* yourself. It is a tremendous blessing that is both exhausting and rewarding. Motherhood is a job where the to-do list is endless— but moms seriously need breaks, too. With four kids ranging in age from four to fourteen, I sometimes feel like I get to the end of the day and have nothing to show for it. I know my efforts as a mother are never in vain, but they can feel overwhelming at times. Have you ever felt that way, Sweet Mama? There are days I feel straight up loony tunes and think, *Man, I need a break!*

When we go for long periods of time without any break from our motherly duties, we begin to show certain signs of wear and tear. Mama, here are some telltale signs you might need a break:

1. You haven't had a shower before 4 p.m. in months, and that's every third day of the week. (Thank goodness for dry shampoo!)

2. You know all the words to every *Daniel Tiger* song and even make up your own versions to get your kids to perform certain tasks. (And it works.)

3. You brush all the kids' teeth as they are racing to get ready for school in the morning but you end up embracing your "sweater tooth" and remedy the potential bad breath with some spearmint chewing gum, just in case you don't make the school drop-off line in time. (Is this one just me? *Ahem.* Guilty "sweater-toother" over here.)

4. What you wear to bed and what you wear to shop for groceries are exactly the same outfit. (Yoga pants and a T-shirt. Yes?)

5. You have locked your keys in the house or the car at least once a week for the past few months. (Just keeping my sweet, patient husband on his toes . . . as well as our friendly neighborhood locksmith.)

6. You follow every request with an "Okay, buddy?" or "Please, sweetie?" even when talking to adults. (Man, I've been so guilty of this one. *Sigh.*)

7. You have looked into how one can erase certain kids' shows from Netflix because you can't stand to hear the theme song from shows like *Pac-Man* or *My Little Pony* one more time without becoming violent and destroying the TV. (Yep. Still don't know how. Any suggestions would be greatly appreciated!)

8. Your idea of a break is a shopping trip, sans kiddos, to Walmart. (It truly is delightful, isn't it?)

9. You automatically drive to the ball field after school even when the kids don't have practice...and stay there to watch the other kids practice. (Score! Snack break!)

10. You often find yourself in the middle of telling a story and completely forgetting what you were talking about in the first place, because you then remember another story that you wanted to talk about but didn't have an adult to tell it to at the time. (The struggle is real...now, what was I writing about?)

11. You have and wear a wide variety of hats because doing your hair is only for "special" occasions, and well, it's just easier to throw on a hat and go...like, every day (one of my fave #momhacks).

12. You refer to watching HGTV's *Beachfront Bargain Hunt* and *Caribbean Life* as "going on vacation." (Just slice me some pineapple and I feel like I'm there! Anybody else?)

13. You take frequent "cat naps"...during the thirty-minute wait in the pickup car line at the elementary school. (What? It's so refreshing. I highly recommend it if you haven't tried it yet.)

14. You watched the Academy Awards only to see who won "Best Animated Film"...because those films were the only ones you had seen that year. (My favorite film was totally robbed this year! *LOL*.)

15. When you say you're going to get some work done in the "office," you walk directly to the bathroom. It's the

only place you won't be followed...well, most of the time. (Yep. *Sigh.*)

16. You often refer to yourself in the third person...and "Mommy" thinks there is nothing at all wrong with that. (*Wink, wink.*)

Sweet Mama, if you can relate to any of these, please, give yourself a break. It's easy to fall into the Mommy Martyrdom trap by simply *resisting* any help that our loved ones and others are trying to offer us. We tell ourselves that we can do it all on our own, and we do it—only to end up exhausted and frustrated that we *had* to do it all on our own. Then, we resent those we love and make derogatory statements about our husbands never helping or family members never being there for us, when deep in our hearts, we know that we intentionally refused their help when they offered it and didn't ask for any help when we actually needed it. We find ourselves bragging to our friends about how much *we* do and how little our family does. We brag about—*ahem*, I mean complain about— not having gone on a date night with our husband in ten years because "we put the kids first." We brag about—I mean rant on and on about—not trusting *anyone* enough to watch our brood because the kiddos would simply go nuts and refuse to allow us a moment to ourselves. We end up playing the "tit-for-tat" game with our husband just so we can make sure he is aware of how much more we do for the kids than he does.

Friends, this is madness. Not only does this rob *us* of peace, it also destroys the peace in our homes and relationships. We must end this destructive cycle and kick this pesky peace pirate to the shore.

So how do we do it? How do we defend ourselves against the Mommy Martyrdom peace pirate? First of all, we must resist the urge to merely "survive," and take a moment each day to feel refreshed and restored so that we can thrive. Sometimes this requires us to arrange our schedules a little differently and even ask for help.

If you are married, sit down with your husband and talk about how you can tweak your schedule and give yourself pockets of peace-building time. Make sure that you have a quiet moment in your day to connect with the Lord by reading His Word and praying. Even if you just focus on memorizing one verse that encourages you in your walk with Him, it will be worthwhile. Get outdoors and go for a walk with your husband or a friend. Join a women's Bible study or interest group that meets regularly. Put some lunches and coffee dates with friends and family on your calendar, so you have something fun to look forward to. Use that mani-pedi gift card that you've been carrying around all year. Plan a nice date night with your hubby. Download some new worship music and listen to it throughout your day.

Friend, these little things are good for the soul. They remind us that motherhood is a big part of who we are, but it is not the whole of who we are. First and foremost, we are daughters of the Living God—loved, cherished, forgiven. Some of us are devoted wives, loving sisters, caretakers of our parents, dependable friends, diligent workers, budding artists, hostesses with the mostest, creative geniuses, solution seekers, and so much more.

Our children are one of the greatest gifts God has given us, but God never intended for us to raise them at the expense of our own peace and relationship with Him. However, He does ask us "to offer your bodies as a living sacrifice, holy and pleasing to God—this is your true and proper worship" (Rom. 12:1). But the Lord gives us so much more than we could ever give Him through our own sacrifices.

I've always been fascinated by the story of God asking Abraham to sacrifice his son, Isaac, on the altar. As a parent, it makes me sick to my stomach to even think about the magnitude of God's request. When I read this story in Genesis 22, I can feel a growing lump in my throat. Abraham and his wife, Sarah, had so desperately wanted children of their own for so many years. God even promised Abraham that he would someday be the father of many nations. Even still, Abraham and Sarah waited for children to come for decades, and she never gave birth to a child. They had all but given up until God fulfilled His promise—like He always does—and brought them Isaac when they were both elderly. I bet they couldn't believe their eyes as Sarah's belly finally began to show life inside it. Isaac's birth was something they weren't sure they would ever experience, and they were probably pinching themselves the entire time. It's such a beautiful story of God doing the miraculous, people keeping the faith, and God delivering on His promise.

As a Jew, Abraham was accustomed to sacrificing an animal for the "burnt offering" as a religious practice to seek atonement for their sins. Remember, this was about two thousand years before the birth of Jesus. So when God asked Abraham to sacrifice his precious son, Isaac, on Mount Moriah, it didn't quite make sense at first. Not only was God asking him to sacrifice a person on the altar, but the person that God asked him to sacrifice was his beloved son! I'm sure that Abraham was so bewildered and confused by it all. Why would God give him the precious boy he and Sarah had longed and prayed for over so many decades only to take the boy from them? What anguish they must have felt! Yet Abraham did as the Lord requested. He held on to the truth that God is always good, and He brought Isaac with him up to the altar on Mount Moriah. I can only imagine how long that trek must have felt. Once at the top, Abraham prepared for the sacrifice and had Isaac climb up on the altar. Can you imagine what Isaac must have been thinking? As Abraham raised the knife, with sweat and tears in his eyes and surely a broken heart, an angel of the Lord commanded Him not to harm the child. The angel went on to say, "Now I know that you fear God, because you have not withheld from me your son, your only son."

What a test! I would like to think that I would have responded like Abraham, but I honestly don't know. Abraham believed that God would provide the sacrificial animal (Gen. 22:8), and He did. Right after the angel told Abraham not to harm Isaac, a ram was caught in a thicket nearby. God provided that ram for Abraham's burnt offering, and Isaac was taken off the altar, alive and well.

The longer I am a parent, the more this story resonates with me. It's pretty crazy, isn't it? There are all sorts of things we can glean from this, and recently, I heard my pastor, Jimmy Evans, explain it in a way that I had never considered before. Pastor Evans said that God was testing Abraham in this way because Isaac had become an object of worship—an idol—in Abraham's life. Isaac was truly the blessing from the Lord that Abraham and Sarah had prayed for, but God never meant for His blessing to become a god in their lives. Wow! I think we can learn a lot from this truth. God doesn't want us to be Mommy Martyrs who center our lives around our children and ultimately make them the object of our worship. We don't sacrifice our lives, our peace, and our relationship with the Lord to and for our children. They are a blessing that God has entrusted to us; they are not God. They can't bring us peace; only God can do that.

God gives parents the responsibility to teach our children about Him and guide them toward a path of peace, but we can do this only with God as the captain of our mothership. He charts the course, and when the waters are murky, He calms our hearts and brings us peace in the midst of the storm.

Two thousand years after God asked Abraham to sacrifice Isaac on Mount Moriah, God sent His one and only Son, Jesus, to the make the greatest sacrifice the world has ever known on a hill called Calvary. Jesus endured false accusations, hateful mockery, physical abuse, and ultimately the cross, and willingly died for all of our sins so that we can live a life of freedom. Thank You, Jesus! His sacrifice gave us a pathway to God's peace. He restored our relationship with the Lord by paying the price for our sins—

which separate us from God. Remember, friend, peace—
shalom—is having wholeness in the Lord. It's His act of
taking us out from under the influence and authority of
chaos and bringing us back under His loving care. All we
have to do is seek Him *first*—His presence, His love, His
approval, His plans, His wisdom, His guidance—and He
will fill our hearts with His perfect peace. Then, and only
then, can we fend off the Mommy Martyrdom peace pirate and effectively pursue, promote, and protect God's
peace in our homes.

A prayer for those struggling with Mommy Martyrdom:

Dear Lord,

*Thank You for sending Your Son, Jesus, as the ultimate
sacrifice. We can never thank You enough for this gift.
Help us to embrace this freedom. You always provide
what we need, right when we need it. Forgive us for placing our kids on a pedestal in our lives. Be the center of
our lives, Lord. We worship You alone. Help us to be intentional about our time, Lord. We want to know You
more, and we want to be at our best for You and for our
family and friends. We know that we can't do this unless
we pursue, promote, and protect Your peace in our lives.
We pray for more peace in our hearts and homes today
and every day, Lord.*

In Jesus' name,
Amen

CHAPTER FIVE

Comparison Chaos

Key Principle: Envy distracts us from the beautiful life that God has specifically given to us.

"I am divorced, so my main anxiety and stress is dealing with the sharing of my sweet boy. I truly believe I was born to be a mom, and it's hard to not get anxious or upset on the inside when people say, 'Oh, but you'll be fiiiiiiine. You'll be able to get things done, clean the house, etc., etc.' I can do that with him, too, thank you. But I know they are not in my shoes, so they could never understand."
—Melissa M., divorced and dating, with one son

When I was about twelve years old, I told my mom that I thought God would make me a mother of boys someday. Boy oh boy, was I right! Having four boys, with no girls in the mix or on the horizon, is somewhat of a novelty.

Believe me, I, too, had to overcome my initial shock at the prospect of so many males in my household.

When I was out and about with my three boys, sporting my huge pregnant belly with my fourth, I received some interesting comments from curious strangers. The obvious first question I would get was, "So are you *finally* having a girl?" When I explained that we were having yet another boy, and this pregnancy would most likely be our last, the responses became somewhat amusing and sometimes downright depressing. After chatting with some fellow moms with sons and gleaning from personal experience, I compiled a list of the Top 10 most ridiculous things that people say to moms of boys:

1. "You're lucky; boys are so much easier than girls." Really? My boys have torn my cornea *five* times...forcing me to wear eye patches...due to engaging in their physical play. I wouldn't consider that *easy*.
2. "Well, boys love their mommies." *Um*. Do girls not love their mommies as well?
3. "Don't worry, you'll have daughters-in-law someday." Yes, we so look forward to embracing our daughters-in-law someday, but that is hardly the same thing as raising a little girl. *Sheesh!*
4. "Bless your heart." Thank you. I will take all the blessings I can get!
5. "Well, aren't you the queen of your household!" Funny, I feel more like a referee...or maybe a monkey trainer.
6. "Be glad you only have boys. You won't have to deal

with as much drama in your home." Please tell that to my emotionally charged eleven-year-old who just cried over not getting the particular Airsoft gun he wanted. I guess it is more of a personality thing than a gender thing.

7. "Boys are so much cheaper than girls." Really? When you add up all the sports fees, hobby costs, and name-brand socks and tennis shoes that boys seem to want these days, boys aren't cheap at all. Oh, did I mention the crazy amount of food consumption in our home?

8. "You'll have so much more peace and quiet when they leave home, because boys don't come around as much...or call." Wow, that's something to look forward to (*tear, sniffle*).

9. "Boys will respect your privacy more." Nope. Mommy's bathroom breaks are their favorite time to chat it up...at least in this season while they are little. Sometimes they even ask to see what's inside the bowl when I'm finished. Yeah, there's no privacy here.

10. "Who's going to look after you when you are old or ill? Maybe you will have a nice daughter-in-law to do the job." Yikes! My husband and I vowed to lean on each other when we are old or sick, but we also want to teach our boys that we each have a responsibility to do our part in caring for others, including aging parents. I certainly don't consider that a female-only role or responsibility.

With all of that said, I love my boys to the moon and back and feel tremendously blessed to have each of them.

I love being their mommy. I'm sure that mothers of girls have heard even crazier statements than these. It's amazing how we are all so quick to place each other in a category, but we are more alike than we realize. Motherhood is a challenge whether you have boys or girls. However, as a community of mothers, we sometimes act like the people who make these silly comments. We make assumptions about each other all the time, right?

I'll be honest. I've struggled with this. I've watched my friends with girls walk through the grocery store at a leisurely rate while their girls quietly hold on to the side of the cart and even help check off the grocery list. Meanwhile, I'm pleading with my little boys to hold my hand and to stop touching everything in the aisle. I've watched my friends with little girls enjoy a sweet day at the library reading time. Their little girls would actually sit and enjoy the story and craft, while my boys were squirmy and asked to go to the bathroom five times... only to have a change of scenery. *Sigh.* I honestly hate to admit this, but I've done it one too many times. I've thought, *Those mothers of girls have it so easy, don't they? Must be nice... and way less embarrassing.* Yep. There's my pride creeping in again, and it is terribly misguided, friend. I know it, and yet I still struggle with it at times.

Gayle O., remarried with twin girls, wrote this to me: "My twins are fourteen, and the middle school years have been the most stressful so far, as the kids in middle school are so judgmental about other kids. The parents seem to be always competing with each other as well. So of course, it stressed me out for my kids as they feel they have to compare and measure up to everyone else. It is very stressful with girls to teach them to be independent and to be their own person and not always comparing themselves to others or how others feel."

Over the years, I've learned the honest truth that boys and girls certainly have some differences, but every child comes with unique gifts *and* challenges of their own. Comparing my children to others is a lost cause, and it only leaves me disappointed in my children and myself as a mom. I can't tell you how many times I've asked my husband if there is something seriously wrong with me or the kids. I would read book after book, try the latest parenting technique, and pray until my knees were sore, to no avail—or at least that's how I saw it at the time. Then, something amazing would happen. Out of the blue, I'd have one of those sweet parenting moments when I could tell that my kids were actually listening to all I had taught them throughout the years. I could actually see things clicking in their minds and hearts by watching their kind actions toward their friends and brothers. If only we could have those kinds of moments every day, but that's simply not the reality we live in.

Sweet Mama, are you worn out? Frustrated? Do you feel like you just can't get it together? Well, you are not alone. I've been there a time or two or three or...maybe a hundred. *Ahem.* Motherhood is awesome. But let's be honest—it can be difficult and frustrating as well.

I got a call from my son's elementary school principal one day last spring. My heart sank when I saw the school's name on my cell phone, but I still answered it with the calmest, cool-as-a-cucumber kind of voice that I could muster. The principal quickly said, "Don't worry. No one is in trouble." *Phew*. Then, she kindly told me that if my son had one more tardy, he would have to go to detention after school. *Ahem*. Oh, man.

I told her that he probably got most of those tardies last week, and she agreed. Yes. My kiddo got four tardies in one week. It was one of *those* weeks, you know? One of those weeks when no matter how much you plan or how hard you try, things just don't seem to go like you want them to. *Argh*. Those weeks are so frustrating.

So how can things get better? Do we just accept them? Well, yes and no. We can't let our frustration win. We must be mindful of what we believe about ourselves, our children, and our job as mamas. Dwelling on lies, temporary truths, or even regret will only make us more frustrated. We've got to cling to what's true and remind ourselves of what a great blessing it is to be a mom. We must remember that this season is temporary. Sometimes, all the craziness of chasing young toddlers, running elementary school kids to ball practice or ballet rehearsals, and making sure teenagers adhere to their curfews can seem like an exhausting cycle with no end in sight. But the truth is this season is temporary. We have these precious kiddos in our home for only a short time. I often hear the saying "The days are long, but the years are short." How true that is! The more we realize this truth, the less likely we will allow our frustration to distract us and steal our joy.

We must also remember that every child makes mistakes—yes, every single child. Whenever my children have been in trouble at school or church, I'm rightfully disappointed in them when they knowingly made a wrong choice. But sometimes, my disappointment turns into full anger because of my pride. I get embarrassed. I mean, that's *my* kiddo who's throwing the fit. That's *my* child who was disrespectful. I start feeling other parents' eyes on me like chicken pox whenever my kids have a meltdown in public. But honestly, that's just my pride messing with me. Every child makes mistakes. When I recognize this truth, I am more likely to approach my children with a graceful heart and less likely to punish them because their actions hurt my pride.

Truth is, there are no perfect parents. This is an important truth. And yet I think most of us have an internal battle with this almost every day. We aren't perfect. None of us are. Not one. We make mistakes. We lose our tempers, raise our voices, and say things we wish we could take back. But the bottom line is that we don't wallow in our past mistakes. We seek God's forgiveness and move forward. We realize that God will forgive our repentant hearts, and He will help us to be the parents we need to be. He will give us the patience, grace, and words we need to raise our children to the best of our abilities.

Worrying about what other people think is *not* going to change anything, and yet I still struggle with worry at times. I've been that parent that wants to crawl into a hole...any available nearby hole, really, anywhere will do...when her child is screaming his head off at the grocery or throwing his food at a restaurant. It's embarrassing. In those moments, I think about how *I* taught him better and *I* don't deserve *this*, and he is making *me* look bad. Yes. Lots of I's and me's in there. So when I step back and really look at the situation, I realize that I'm so upset because my melting-down child is a real kick to my pride as a parent. Yes, that word again.

Can you relate? One or two or even three bad public incidents with our children don't mean that we are a bad parent. And who cares what the apparent onlookers think? Honestly, most of them are probably wishing they could do something to help and reflecting on their own experiences with children being difficult. Believe me, sister, we aren't alone in our struggle. Let's not worry about what "so-and-so" thought when little Jimmy burped out loud at the restaurant the other day. Worry only steals our joy and makes us lose focus on what's important. Sometimes this means we step away for a few minutes before we lose our cool and say something hurtful. Every now and then, we may need to seek advice from a doctor, counselor, or parenting book to learn how to discipline each unique child the best we can. There will be lots of mistakes on the way—by us and by our children. This doesn't mean that we stop trying.

Our kids will eventually get it right. This may sound like some kind of singsong, "Kumbaya" statement, but honestly, our kids *will* get it right. Proverbs 22:6 says, "Train up a child in the way he should go; even when he is old he will not depart from it" (ESV). Parenting is one of the most worthwhile and important things we will ever do. We can't lose hope. We must realize that we are training our children to live God-honoring, self-sustaining, joy-filled lives. And this is a *long* process. You have to take the long view.

Just because we have a frustrating day or month or year doesn't mean that our kids will never get it right. We must *believe* in them, *pray* for them, and *keep teaching* them every single day. I love the promise of Proverbs 29:17: "Discipline your son [or daughter], and he will give you *rest*; he will give *delight* to your heart" (ESV, emphasis mine).

We are all works in progress, and every day we are hopefully getting closer to becoming the mom God wants us to be. The details of this "becoming" will look a little different for each of us, but the big picture is very similar. As Christian women, we've been set free from the standard of this world. Look at Romans 12:2 for help: "Do not conform to the pattern of this world, but be transformed by the renewing of your mind. Then you will be able to test and approve what God's will is—His good, pleasing and perfect will."

Unfortunately, comparison has become part of the fabric of our modern society, and social media perpetuates this twenty-four/seven. Friend, please don't get me wrong here; I'm a huge fan of social media, but we must be careful not to let it swallow us up. We must understand that moms on Facebook rarely share their worst pictures or embarrassing moments. Ninety-nine percent of the time, we're looking at each other's highlights of the day. Think about it. Why do we beat ourselves up that our friend's kid got the math award, and ours didn't even get on the honor roll? We see these highlight posts, and we allow them to ruin our otherwise great day and take the wind out of our mommy sails. Or we're the ones proudly boasting about our kids' accolades, and we let the "likes" and comments puff us up and make us feel like "mom of the year." The pendulum swings both ways, and it's easy to get caught in the chaos of comparison. But it's a dangerous place to be.

When we allow ourselves to get caught in the comparison trap, peace pirates invade our space and plunder our sanity and contentment. Comparison steals our joy and patience and replaces those with bitterness and frustration. The chaos that ensues around comparison often rids us of self-control, and we open ourselves up to angry interactions with our snarky countenance. When we give ourselves over to comparison, we put ourselves smack-dab in the middle of a race that we can *never* win, because the path and rules are always changing. Comparison is a pesky peace pirate that we must swiftly push overboard the minute we feel it creeping in. We can do this only when we stay grounded in prayer and ask the Lord to help us to take these thoughts of comparison captive and replace them with the truth of His Word.

Recently, I was waiting in the checkout line at the grocery store and browsing magazine covers. As I was scanning each cover, one in particular caught my eye. I couldn't believe what I saw. It had various pictures of Hollywood moms with ratings, like A– or D+, next to their names. These were action shots of them doing normal, everyday things with their kids, mind you. Some of these pictures had subtitles accusing the mom of yelling too much or rushing her children. Others showed more flattering photos of a star mom kissing her baby, all while looking fabulous, and she was dubbed sweet and caring.

As I stood there, with my mouth gaping open out of sheer disgust, I realized that I was giving this cover way too much attention, just as that magazine company was probably hoping I, and many other moms, would. If we are honest with ourselves, we have done this to our mommy friends on occasion. No, we probably haven't said it out loud or written it down, but we have said it in our minds loud and clear. I think that sometimes we have this unspoken mommy gauge keeping score in our minds when we think things like: *My goodness, Cindy sure gripes at her kids a lot, and they kind of act like monkeys. She probably didn't read enough of that book that we all know we are supposed to read that clearly explains how to be the perfect parent with step-by-step instructions along with pictures and details on how to handle every kind of child, personality, home situation, and dilemma. Wow, I am so glad I did!*

Or we might think...*Please, stop staring at me and my crazy kids! I can't control them. Why can't they act like Sheri's kids? She and her husband sure trained them right. Why didn't I read that book that we all know we are supposed to read that clearly explains how to be the perfect parent with step-by-step instructions along with pictures and details on how to handle every kind of child, personality, home situation, and dilemma? I am sure they did.*

Either way, we aren't doing ourselves any favors, and we certainly aren't helping each other. Honestly, I think all moms would benefit from more encouraging words and less stares. Gawking eyes have *never* made me a better mom, and if anything, they've made me feel more insecure and a little *ca-ray-zee*, if you know what I mean.

A few years ago, I wanted to go to one of my favorite discount stores to buy some additional Christmas decorations...yes, I am one of those who thinks Christmas can't get here fast enough. After a pretty frustrating day, I decided that I was going to turn the day around by taking my six-year-old, Connor, and sleepy two-year-old, Chandler, along. I started getting Chandler out of his car seat and into the stroller, and suddenly, he became a contortionist (a pretty gifted one actually...like on the level of a future gymnast or Cirque de Soleil performer). There was no way I could get him in there. So I did what any good mom does. I started telling him that he will *not* do this and he *must* get into his stroller right *now*. And suddenly, he looked at me and said, *I'm so sorry, Mother, I will sit down.* Then, we had the best time shopping together! Uh, no, not really. Instead, he bent his back and kicked his legs, and said "No, Mommy! No!" Meanwhile, Connor was waiting impatiently beside the van saying, "Can we go in now?"

I continued with Chandler, when I suddenly realized that another mom was standing there audaciously gawking at me—no smile, no anything, just gawking. I snapped. I put Chandler back in his car seat, told Connor to get back in the car, collapsed the stroller, and slammed the trunk closed with an intense "I am not doing this right now!" I think I probably threw the spy mom a sinister smile and a quiet "You're welcome to feel better about *your* parenting now" expression. It was not one of my more patient or nicer moments, and I left feeling defeated and totally embarrassed.

When we feel another mom's eyes burning like lasers through our backs, we get nervous and feel judged, and then we start this kind of "mommy war." We think, *Okay, that was bad, but I am not as bad as* _____. Is that really how we are supposed to evaluate our mom skills? I don't think so, but I am guilty of it, too.

I saw this kind of comparison trap played out to an extreme a few years ago. It was all over the news and social media—terrifying footage of a four-year-old boy falling into a gorilla cage exhibit at the Cincinnati Zoo and being pulled around by Harambe, a gorilla who unfortunately had to be shot to keep the child safe. It's horrific and gut-wrenching to watch. And I'm sad that the gorilla had to die. But the real issue that was brought to a blazing light through this story was the rampant mom-shaming. Over the course of a few days, I saw countless posts about how terrible that mother was or how she was solely responsible for having Harambe killed. There were so many toxic comments full of hate and judgment plastered all over the internet. This incident was a nightmare for this family, the zoo, and all the bystanders. Terrible! I can't even imagine what that family went through . . . not to mention the huge backlash. No one wanted it to happen. This poor mother and child went through so much turmoil. She will carry this nightmare with her forever. She felt the daggers in her back and heard all the scathing comments ringing in her ears.

As a mother of four boys, I can honestly say that I could see this incident happening to us. We, too, have a rambunctious four-year-old boy who is as inquisitive and energetic as Curious George. I know that he could have jumped that fence and found himself in the same nightmare lickety-split. Just the thought of it sends shivers down my spine.

Are we too prideful as a society to assume that this kind of nightmare can't happen to *us*? I'm not a perfect parent, and I've yet to find one. God is the only perfect parent. My goodness, even Joseph and Mary lost Jesus for *three days* and in a *foreign land* (Luke 2:43–47). The parents of the Son of God (we will talk more about this later)! I take comfort in this. I'm relieved to know that I'm not alone in my struggle to be a good parent—to raise my kids right and, yes, to keep a close eye on them. But I'm imperfect. I make mistakes. And apparently, Jesus' parents did, too.

When we feel pride rising up in us and we are tempted to shame another mother, we need to remember Jesus' famous words to the crowd furiously wanting to stone a woman. In John 8:7, He said this: "He that is without sin among you, let him first cast a stone at her" (KJV). If there had been a mic to drop back in those days, then He would've dropped it for sure. Instead of judging another mom (and anyone else for that matter), let's offer up a prayer for her and her family. I think that's what Jesus would do.

In Luke 11:46, Jesus is addressing the pious Pharisees over their judgmental behavior and says, "And you experts in the law, woe to you, because you load people down with burdens they can hardly carry, and you yourselves will not lift one finger to help them." This is sobering when I think about how I have been on both sides of the mommy wars and have sometimes acted as a Pharisee rather than Christ-like when I have seen a mom in crisis.

When we see a stressed-out mom at her wit's end, why can't our first inclination be to offer her some help or an encouraging word? If she is trying to push a high chair to the table at a restaurant while juggling multiple kids, we can help her get the high chair to the table. If she's pushing a cart up an incline in a supermarket parking lot along with a screaming baby, let's help her get the cart to her car and unload her groceries while she soothes the baby. I can't tell you how many times the "I have been there" smile from a fellow mom has calmed me down and made me laugh instead of cry. Every mom has been there, and if you honestly have no idea what I am talking about right now, just wait. It's coming. I say that in the most compassionate way possible, Sweet Mama.

Someone once said, "Mothering is not for the faint of heart." Yeah, that's the understatement of the century! It's tough. So let's be burden-lifters instead of burden-builders. Besides, our families are the ones who benefit the most from a calmer, cooler mom who is doing the best she can and not worrying about what any other mom thinks. And in case you haven't heard this in a while, please know that you are an *amazing* child of God, and He will never give you more than you can handle with His help, including your role as mother and friend of mothers. So how about it? Let's stop trying to mother in our own strength and instead surrender our hearts and homes to the Lord. Let's end these "mommy wars" for good.

Let's stop comparing our weaknesses and celebrate our

strengths instead. I believe each of us possesses a slice of mommy wisdom that stands out from the rest. Over the years, I've learned a lot from observing my friends navigate motherhood with their unique strengths, and it's made me a better mom.

No two mothers are exactly the same. We all come from different backgrounds and upbringings. Our husbands have different personalities, and some of us aren't currently married due to different circumstances. I love the diversity. Sometimes, I stand in awe of my various mommy friends, and think, *Why can't I be like her?* But then I remember...I am my own kind of wife and mother—specifically designed for my husband and four boys. I'm perfectly imperfect for each one of them. Even so, I've learned a thing or two from moms that do things a little different from me. They help me to see things from a different perspective, and this makes me *better* at mothering—when I allow it to. So here are ten amazing mamas who encourage me to be a better mom:

1. The Label-Maker Mama: This mom is one who loves labeling everything. She is a master organizer and color-codes everything. If you ask her where something is, you bet your bottom dollar she knows exactly where to find it...and all the accessories you need with it. She challenges me to see organization as my friend. She reminds me that taking the time to organize my things will ultimately give me more time to spend doing more of what I love with those I love. I'm thankful for this mom in my life.

2. The Planner Mom: This mom always knows what's on the agenda for the day—because she made the agenda. She is a leader and great at event planning. This lady is the room mom—or better yet, president of the PTA. Whenever I have a question about a school event, I can always count on her. With four kiddos, each with different schedules, I need to be more like this mama more than ever. But thankfully, she's always there to remind me about the field trips and homework project due dates.

3. The Free-Spirit Mama: I long to be more like this mom, because she has fun with her kids wherever she takes them. They could be in a doctor's waiting room, and she will come up with an interesting and fun game to entertain them while they wait. If the baby is snot-faced and crying, she's not rattled. She just wipes the nose and breastfeeds the baby—cover or not. She does what needs to be done and shakes off what anyone else thinks. I *love* that about this mom. She embraces her kiddos for who they are . . . not who she wants them to be.

4. The All-Natural Mom: This mom takes a shower, puts on some comfortable clothes, fixes her hair into a bun, applies some lip balm, and is out the door. She radiates natural beauty. She doesn't like makeup, but she loves essential oils and probably has an oil for any and every ailment. This mom has her own vegetable garden and frequently makes fresh meals from it . . . and shares some veggies with her friends and neighbors. She is environmentally conscious and likes to buy only organic products and foods for her family. I love how this

mom is amazing at educating other moms on the natural options that are at our fingertips. She inspires me
to think about what I use to clean my home and what
kinds of products I use on my skin. And I always like
it when she teaches me how to make my own sugar
scrubs, soaps, and candles.

5. The Creative Mom: This mama can make almost any-
    thing with her hands, and she's always thinking outside
    the box. When it comes to her kids' birthday parties,
    she knocks it out of the park. From the food, to the
    decorations, to the cake, to the goody bags—she al-
    ways makes her guests feel special and like they have
    escaped to another land. It's awesome. She makes jew-
    elry, clothes, artistic pieces, pottery—you name it and
    she can usually make it. She challenges me to broaden
    my own creativity, and she inspires her kids to foster
    their imaginations.

6. The Handy Mom: I'd love for this mama to make me a
    harvest table. This mom knows her way around a tool
    shed, and her favorite kinds of gifts are those that fit in
    her tool belt. She's not afraid to get dirty, and she loves
    the smell of sawdust. She pretty much built her kids'
    bunk beds, and she's always got a home improvement
    project going on. Instead of buying a new piece of furni-
    ture, she'd much rather refinish it or build it herself. She's
    a hardworking, self-taught mama who always has a drill
    close by. I wish I had her skills . . . and tool collection.

7. The Honest Mommy: Ever have one of those days
    when you feel like you are the *only* one whose kids
    are nuts? Well, have no fear, the honest mom will help

you to regain your sanity every time. This mom has a way of relating to just about everyone. She's refreshingly raw in the hardships of motherhood. She never shames those whose kiddos are less than perfect. Instead, she grabs your hand, looks you in the eye, and says, "Been there, too, Sweet Mama. This is hard right now, but it will get better."

8. The Fit Mom: This mom is full of energy. When she found out she was pregnant, her first purchase was a running stroller. This mom looks amazing, and she works hard for it. She loves exercising and even teaches aerobics classes. This mama makes her kiddos kale shakes in the morning and takes them on a family jog after dinner. She invites her friends and family to work out with her. She'd rather walk with a friend than go out to lunch. Her smile and confidence are infectious, and she challenges me to be more health conscious— not just to look better, but to feel better. This mom is a natural-born encourager and cheerleader, and she's a great friend to have in your corner.

9. The Punctual Mom: I need to pick this mama's brain. She's never late and usually a little early. This mom lays out clothes the night before and sets multiple alarms to make sure everyone gets up on time. She has a set of snacks, coloring books, and child-friendly electronics in the car, so she can keep the kids happy getting from place to place or while they wait...since they arrive early wherever they go. And she's always eager to share these prep packs with other moms who failed to plan and are running late...like me.

10. The Thankful Mama: This mama longed to have children for years. She struggled to find the *one*...to get pregnant...to sustain her pregnancy. After years of wondering if she'd ever hear someone call her "Mom," *it* happened. She exudes thankfulness for every single moment—as if motherhood is a dream come true. Honestly, I need more of her in my life, and I crave her perspective. Motherhood *is* a dream come true. It's a privilege and a calling. Every moment—even the messy, loud, chaotic, exhausting, irritating, and well, downright loony tunes moments—is a gift. It is good to be reminded of this truth from time to time.

There are most definitely more than ten, because each and every mother is amazing in her own way. All of us! You probably saw a little bit of yourself in all of these, right? None of us is simply *one* kind of mom; we're a kaleidoscope of strengths. We just have to stop comparing ourselves to each other long enough to see it, and embrace our own strengths as a wife and a mom. This is especially hard to do when we fail to see the beauty in our own trench, because each day seems to have more trouble than the day before. It's hard not to grow bitter when our marriage is rocky, and we can't seem to get on the same page with our spouse. How are we supposed to stay positive when everything about our parenting feels negative at the moment? The truth is that each and every one of us will experience difficulty and trouble within our lifetime. It is part of being human. Jesus said so. John 16:33 states, "I have told you these things, so that in me you may have peace. In this world you will have trouble. But take heart! I have overcome the world."

Whether big or small, our troubles often cause us to question the way things are and maybe even get caught in the habit of comparing our lives to our perception of how others live. I have certainly asked, "Why?" from a place of shallow jealousy when comparing myself to a friend. Maybe you can relate. Have you ever asked yourself any of these questions?

Why her and not me?

Her kids adore her, listen well, and make her proud. My kiddos constantly embarrass me with their behavior, and I just feel overwhelmed and enraged. I wish my kids would respond to me like hers do.

Why do I have to do everything around this house?

Can't anyone lend a hand or simply not leave their underwear on the floor? There's not a day that I don't see my neighbor's kids and husband working hard on their yard. Must be nice!

Why is it so easy for her?

She always looks so fit, and she usually eats whatever she wants. I gain a pound every time I so much as glance at a cupcake. She's so lucky... and skinny. I am, well... not.

Why can't I afford to get my nails done . . . and a pedicure . . . and a massage?

Her nails always look so pretty. What I wouldn't give to live with her budget!

I realize these thoughts are petty and fleeting, and they can change by the hour. These are details that don't really matter in the grand scheme of things. More or less, they are simply annoying, self-serving distractions that leave us feeling less than satisfied with ourselves and our lives, when we just need to be thankful. If you are anything like me, you tend to ponder these questions all too often. Frankly, we just need to stop this and move on. Thankfulness helps us cultivate and keep a peace-filled perspective, which will lead us to have a more peaceful disposition.

There is another level of "Why?" that we are reluctant to face. It's the kind of "Why?" that takes our breath away, stops us in our tracks, and terrifies us. It makes us question all that we hold dear and even the goodness or existence of God. Pondering this kind of "Why?" forces us to explore our worst fears. "What If?" often follows and even keeps us up at night. These questions look more like this . . .

Why her and not me?

We got pregnant the minute I stopped taking the pill, and she hasn't been able to conceive even after undergoing in vitro fertilization three times and losing four babies to miscarriages.

Why her and not me?

Her husband seems to adore her, while mine will barely look my way. Is my husband having an affair?

Why her and not me?

She has it all together. She's beautiful, friendly, and successful. I can barely get out of bed due to my ongoing bout with depression. This dark cloud just won't go away.

Why her and not me?

She was adopted and raised in a beautiful, loving home, and I was tossed from foster home to foster home. I guess nobody wanted me.

Why her and not me?

My family has to move into the Ronald McDonald House while our young daughter is receiving multiple rounds of chemotherapy and fighting for her precious life. Her kids have barely had to go to the doctor.

Why her and not me?

Why? Why? Why????

There is nothing petty or fleeting about these "Whys" at all. They make our hearts ache. The hurt they cause cuts

us to our very core. The "What Ifs" they bring are paralyzing to our souls. Again, we must remember John 16:33.
Jesus acknowledges that every single last one of us will have
trouble in this life, but we *will* overcome it because He has
overcome the world, the very place that brings us trouble.
We live in a place that isn't perfect, but we have a perfect Savior. Our lives can never be nor will they ever be
without flaws, snags, and detours. Life is messy. There is so
much blessing and so much pain, all happening at the same
time.

So the next time we are fearful of a dire circumstance
that has hit one of our friends, or we find that we are dis-
satisfied with our lives in comparison to our perceptions of
another's life, what are we supposed to do? We can reach
out and be present with our friends. We can be honest and
talk through our feelings with our husband. We can offer
to help our friend in need by making a meal or watching
her kids. We don't have the power to change our friend's
heartbreaking situation, and many times our hands are tied
to change our own predicament. But there's one thing we
can do that is our very lifeline, especially in times of trouble. We can pray.

We can pray for our friend who is hurting. Pray that
God will give her peace and strength to face her difficult
situation. We can pray that God will surround her with
friends and family who can offer support. We can pray that
God will help us to see how we can help her in a tangible
way. We can pray for ourselves. Pray that God will help us
to see the blessings in our lives and not be paralyzed by the
"What Ifs" and "Whys." We can pray that God will give us

strength when we are facing trouble and provide a peace that surpasses understanding along the way. We can pray that we won't fall apart when trouble comes, but instead we will remember that Jesus overcame the grave and He will help us overcome any hardship.

I honestly can't think of any time in my life when comparing myself to others made my situation better. Prayer, on the other hand, has calmed my soul and helped me to see beyond myself.

Let's remind ourselves daily to stop comparing and start praying. Tell the "Whys" and "What Ifs" to take a hike!

A prayer for those caught in the comparison trap:

Dear Lord,

Help us to remember that You have created the only standard that matters when it comes to my role as wife and mom. I am not perfect, but You have chosen and equipped me to be a loving wife to my husband and mom to my precious kiddos. Please help me to stop comparing myself and my life to others. Help me to set my mind and heart on You and Your standard.

In Jesus' name,
Amen

CHAPTER SIX

Clenching Control

Key Principle: We love our family best when we acknowledge that God is in control, not us.

"Overall, the biggest stress for me as a mom is feeling like a failure . . . My fear of disappointing [my son], or even failing him, is a target on my back that Satan loves to take advantage of."

—Ashley B., married mom of one

I rolled the windows down and felt the warmth of brilliant sunbeams shooting through the fluffy white clouds in the sky. I turned up some festive music on the car radio and strapped my kids into their car seats. I was determined to make the day a good one. After all, I had planned accordingly. The kids were out of school for the day, and I so desperately wanted to spend some sweet time with all of them together. My husband had to work that day, so I decided to take a mini road trip with my four crazy boys—all by myself—to Stone Mountain Park. It's a really fun spot about two hours from where we live. There's a splash area, a train, fun shows, a huge barn with multiple levels where you can shoot foam balls at each other from afar, loads of yummy food, and even a suspended high-climbing area—*everything* a kid loves to do, right? What could possibly go wrong? I had everything under control. This day was going to be epic!

The trip started off just fine. The boys seemed pretty excited to be out of school and off on a little adventure. I even put on one of their favorite movies in the portable DVD player, and I purchased an enormous bag of Doritos for the journey—waaaay more than they could possibly consume.

We were buzzing down the road, everyone happy and chill. This trip was going to be awesome. Then, about an hour into our journey, one of my sons decided to open the bag of chips. Everything went downhill from there. My eldest son, Cooper, who was around ten at the time, felt like it was his duty to dole out the chips to everyone. Of course, that didn't sit well with his younger brothers. I told Cooper to be fair and give everyone about ten chips to start off with. He begrudgingly started to do so. Then Chandler, who was four going on twenty-five, got a death grip on the bag and claimed that Cooper hadn't given him the correct number of chips. So Cooper decided that Chandler could no longer have *any* chips because he hadn't been patient enough. Isn't it funny how disciplinary our children can become to their younger siblings? Hmm.

Meanwhile, I was trying to drive safely and keep my eyes on the road. I was determined to stay calm and not let myself morph into a pirate mom. I wanted this day to be a win for all of us, and I didn't want my anger to ruin it. I told the boys to "work it out" and "be nice." Yeah. That didn't work.

Unfortunately, the bag fiasco carried on to the point that it became a literal tug-of-war between Cooper and Chandler. Chatham, who was eighteen months at the time, started fussing and saying, "Chippies, pwease! Chippies!" Connor, the peacemaker of the bunch, who was eight at the time, was pleading with them to let go of the bag and saying, "Guys! Just stop fighting."

God bless that sweet boy.

The arguing and complaining got so loud that it drowned out the happy music I had strategically put on the radio, to the point my ears started ringing. At that moment, I'd had enough of their crazy shenanigans. In an effort to keep my fleeting composure, I calmly said, "Cooper, give Chandler the chips so he can give himself what he needs and pass them on." Then, I waited for a response. I am their mom after all, and I needed to get this car back in order and regain control. However, Cooper and Chandler continued to fight. I said it a little louder. Nothing happened. My blood began to boil, and I started to feel the pirate mom raging inside me. "Give him the chips!" I shouted.

"No," Cooper responded. "He can't have them because he's not being patient."

Really, Cooper? We're seriously going to get all high and mighty about this particular issue *now*?

"Cooper, give him the chips, *now!*" I responded sharply. Again, nothing.

Friends, this is where I lost it. I'm not sure where all of my composure went, but it left me for sure. I was so angry at their disobedience, arguing, and complaining. All I could think about was how *they* were out of control and how *they* were ruining my plans. I pulled the car over, whipped my head around like in *The Exorcist,* and with great intensity and volume and crazy eyes, I blurted out, "*Give! Him! The! Chips!*"

Silence. Which was honestly the best thing I'd heard in an hour. But after about a minute, the kids burst into laughter. "I'm sorry, Mom," Cooper said. "I didn't know you were soooo mad. Here's the chips, Chandler."

"Mom, you're so mad, and it's funny!" Chandler replied with a goofy grin.

"Yeah! Mommy said, 'Give! Him! The! Chips!' [with Chandler's best growly voice, which was a pretty good impression of me at that moment, honestly]."

I stared at them through the rearview mirror for a minute and tried to calm myself down. After some time, I started giggling, too. I knew this whole road trip had been a bust, and it turned all of us into raging lunatics. I thought I had everything under control. I had planned everything, started the journey with a good attitude, and tried to make this a memorable experience for all of us. Well, I achieved the last one of those, but not in the way I had hoped. Stubbornness, arguing, and complaining took over my minivan, and it took my patience and peace with it. And I went all Cujo on my kids. *Sigh.*

I lost control. Control of my agenda. My hopes for the day. My kids' behavior. My own sanity.

You better believe that when we got home those kiddos had some unpleasant consequences and loss of privileges due to their disrespectful behavior. The laughter and ensuing "mad mommy" impressions were good medicine for us all at the time, but deep in my heart, I felt like a failure. I felt so frustrated with my kids and myself. On the drive home, so many questions filled my mind... *Why won't they listen and obey me all the time? Why don't they get along all the time? Why can't I maintain control of my kids, my composure, and my agenda all the time? Why is this so hard?*

Maybe you can relate, Sweet Mama. If you've been a mom for any length of time, you know that control is really a big stinkin' illusion. However, most of us still try to convince ourselves that we just need to hold on tighter to our loved ones, and we will somehow have control over them. We're convinced that this longing for total control is a motherly and even Godly quest.

Friends, control is the biggest peace pirate of them all, and it greatly damages our relationships. When we try to clench control and realize that we're losing our grasp, it causes us a lot of worry and anxiety. However, when we think that we've totally got our kids and home under control, we can become prideful and judgmental. Both of these dynamics will deplete us of peace, and both result in worry. And worry is deeply rooted in fear.

Paul tells us in 2 Timothy 1:7 that God doesn't give us a spirit of fear, and yet many, if not most, of us worry about our children and our effectiveness as a mother. It keeps us up at night, and it's paralyzing. We tell ourselves that worrying about our children is okay because it's a way of loving them and showing concern, but Jesus tells us otherwise. 1 John 4:18 says, "There is no fear in love. But perfect love drives out fear, because fear has to do with punishment. The one who fears is not made perfect in love."

There is so much we can learn about motherhood from this one verse. First of all, when we fear for or worry about our children, we are not doing this out of love. Rather, it's out of punishment. However, as I read this verse as it relates to motherhood, the punishment of fear is against *ourselves* first. We grasp at control so tightly to prove to ourselves—and to the world—that we are good moms with everything in its place and everyone doing what they are supposed to do. And when everything falls apart—and it inevitably will—we feel defeated. We punish *ourselves* and wallow in shame, anxiety, and frustration just as the enemy would like us to do. Then we turn our eyes to the very subjects who let us down and made us look bad: our offspring. They're the ones out of line, right? So we make them pay for their sins with our nasty tone, impatient responses, frigid countenance, and overwhelming negativity. And before we even realize it, this peace pirate has plundered our heart and home and set sail in victory.

Sweet Mama, I know the destruction of control, and tragically, I have let this peace pirate steal too much of my time, my sanity, and my relationships with my children. So how do we defeat it? First, we must recognize that our need for control is wrecking our lives and homes, and understand which dynamic of control we are struggling with.

The Pride of Control

I love my friend Ally. She's hilarious, unfiltered, and as generous as they come. When we first met, she had two girls. One in elementary and one in middle school. At the time, I had two boys in elementary school. We attended the same church, and I remember seeing how nicely she would stroll into church with her husband and girls every Sunday. The girls were dressed to the nines and sweetly holding Ally's hands, with smiles on their faces. I remember being so jealous. *Why in the world can't my boys act that way?* Most Sundays, I was trying to wrangle my boys into church while they were chasing each other with a booger on their pointer finger. Their clothing was seriously the least of my worries. If they were dressed in clean clothes, I considered it a win.

A few years down the road, I had coffee with Ally and told her that I was pregnant with my third child. Being an extremely honest friend, she nearly spit out her coffee and said, "Girl, *why*? Your boys are crazy. I don't know why in the world you want to add one more!"

I laughed. Her answer was so her, and I knew she meant well by it. Well, a couple of months later, Ally called me and said *she* was pregnant. I was thrilled. There's nothing sweeter than being pregnant at the same time as one of your friends. Six months later, I had my third son, Chandler, and a couple months after that, she had her first son, Bobby. She was totally freaked out that he was a boy, but she figured he would be "good" like her daughters. She took pride in being a pretty strict disciplinarian, and she was confident she could raise her son in the same way. She had no clue what was in store for her.

Over the next couple of years, Ally and I would get our boys together for playdates, and she would express to me how Bobby was more difficult than her girls had been. He wouldn't listen the first time, and he didn't seem the least bit peeved when he had to sit in time-out due to his behavior. The older he was, the more defiant he became. Until one day, Ally had her mother-in-law watch Bobby for a few hours, and she received a terrifying call. At only two years old, Bobby had unbolted the back door and gone outside to the trampoline all by himself. When his grandma went out to get him, he climbed down and ran into the house like a lightning bolt, and locked the door. Ally's mother-in-law's heart began to race as she pleaded with Bobby to unlock the door. She ran around to the front of the house, but that door was locked, too. She was stuck outside with no key, no cell phone, and no way to get to Bobby. She began to panic, while Bobby stared out the window, completely amused. Finally, Ally's mother-in-law found a neighbor who was home, and she was able to call Ally and tell her what was happening. Ally rushed to the house and unlocked the door only to find a calm and collected Bobby watching television. There was also evidence that he had climbed up on the kitchen counter to get various snacks. Ally was relieved that Bobby was okay but also furious that he had been so defiant and put his poor grandma through one of the most terrifying and frustrating days of her life.

I remember Ally telling me the story with tears in her eyes. "Girl, I don't know how in the world you stay sane with your boys," she said. "I used to think I had parenting figured out because my girls have always been so well behaved, for the most part. I used to kinda judge other parents whose kids always seemed a little out of hand. I honestly thought that my husband and I simply must be better parents than most. Well, Bobby has showed me how wrong I was. Sometimes, I'm at a loss at how to handle him, even though I feel like I've got things under control with my girls. I love Bobby so much, but he has just about driven me crazy with his strong will."

Have you ever felt that way? You think you've got this motherhood thing in the bag, and then life shifts a bit, and you find yourself desperately grasping for control like searching for a water source in the desert—only to find out that it was a mirage all along.

The Panic of Control

My third son, Chandler, is a riot. He honestly came out of the womb smiling and flashing his huge dimples. And I am such a sucker for dimples, which is a good thing because this child has just about driven me crazy these last six years—and he is only six. He has always been a screamer, whether he was happy or sad, and he can achieve an impressive decibel level. He is naturally a loud person, so wherever we go, he tends to draw attention. Even so, he is truly a darling boy. He has a zest for life like no one I've ever known, and he is super smart. So when we enrolled him for preschool, I had no reservations. Sure, he's a little loud and wiggly, but what preschool boy isn't, right?

Fast-forward a couple months. I went to pick him up in the car line, and his teacher angrily plopped him down in his car seat. She was clearly frustrated, so I decided to ask her if everything was okay. She gave me a look of frustration that I had never seen on her face before. This wasn't the kind you get from just one difficult day. I could tell that it had been building up for a long time. She proceeded to tell me that Chandler had had a bad day and that he'd ended the day by going, "Pew, pew, pew!" making little gun motions with his hands. She said she couldn't tolerate this kind of behavior. I agreed that Chandler knew better, and told her I would talk to him about it. As I drove away, my heart sank. I hadn't received any notes home or had any calls from the school, but Chandler clearly wasn't doing well in his class.

I decided to set up a conference with the teacher to get a clearer picture. She suggested I come and observe Chandler in class before the conference, so I did. I showed up without letting Chandler know about it. When I walked in, he was literally in a chair facing the corner. The teacher explained that he was in time-out for playing too rough with one of the little girls in class. After his time-out, they had a craft. During the craft, they were supposed to paint inside the lines of an apple drawing. The teacher reprimanded Chandler for painting outside the lines, and he pushed the paper away in frustration. In circle time, Chandler had a hard time staying on his carpet square, and he got angry when the teacher didn't call on him to answer one of the questions. As I watched all the other kids sit pretty quietly on their squares while Chandler wiggled about, I could see why his teacher felt like Chandler was a disruption.

During their lunch time, she and I finally had our conference. She explained that she just "couldn't figure Chandler out." Again, my heart sank. As a former teacher, all I could hear was, "Your child is a nuisance—weirdo—distraction." Even though she chose her words carefully, I could see her exhaustion with my son.

When I took Chandler home that day, I had tears in my eyes. I asked him why he had such a hard time sitting on his carpet square and why he was playing rough with that little girl, and why he couldn't just listen and paint inside the lines. All he could say was, "I never get any stars on the good behavior chart. She never sees me doing good things." My mama heart sank even lower. Here I was, rightfully frustrated with my son and his disobedient and sometimes disruptive behavior, but I was totally overlooking another side of this. Maybe he was right. Maybe his teacher had been so put off by my son and his disobedience at the beginning of the year that she wasn't seeing the good in him.

So I made it my mission to change her perspective. I made several doctors' appointments to get Chandler evaluated, in order to make sure we weren't missing some underlying attention, learning, or medical issue. We found nothing. But Chandler was still struggling with his behavior at school. Our doctor suggested that we see an occupational therapist who specialized in behavior. I didn't know much about OT at the time, but it turned out to be a huge blessing for us. Over those few months, I saw great improvement in Chandler's behavior at home, and the principal at the school said he was doing better as well. The occupational therapist even put Chandler in school scenarios like circle time and lunch time to reinforce proper behavior. Chandler gained confidence in knowing how to respond in an appropriate way, and I was so relieved that we had found something that helped both of us make improvements.

However, his teacher still seemed exasperated by him, and Chandler's improvements didn't seem to matter to her. Every school day, he would get in the van and tell me how he thought he had a good day but didn't get any stars on the good behavior chart. This broke my heart. When I asked the teacher about it, she just said, "He'll get there." I felt so defeated. I remember crying a lot that year, and I felt like a failure as a parent. On the one hand, I assumed the teacher thought I, as a mother, hadn't done a good job raising Chandler up to that point. But on the other hand, I felt like I was totally failing Chandler by not convincing his teacher to see the good in him. Those months were maddening, and my peace was waning.

I know this teacher probably didn't realize how closely Chandler was examining his chart and how negatively the absence of stars beside his name affected him. And just to be clear, she never said anything unkind or raised her voice at Chandler. Believe me, I asked him on a regular basis. The problem was that she just couldn't see past his strong-willed and often loud demeanor. She didn't quite know how to take him or how to bring out the best in him because she couldn't *see* the best in him. And the truth is, no matter how much therapy he had, or how many doctor's appointments I took him to, or how many notes I sent to her, or how many parent-teacher conferences we had, I had absolutely no control over her view of my son. Not one iota. I also had to realize that I didn't have complete control over my son and his behavior. He is a human being with a mind of his own. As his parent, I am his primary teacher and guide. The rest is up to the Lord.

I realized that I had to surrender my feelings, my son's behavior, and his teacher's opinion of my son to the Lord on a daily basis, or I would allow this peace pirate to throw us overboard.

My husband, Dave, always reminds me that we, as parents, take way too much blame for our kids' failures and way too much glory for their triumphs. It is our job to model good behavior for our kids, to guide them, to teach them, and to discipline them as well. However, they are not robots. They have sinful tendencies just like all of us. They want to be in control, and sometimes their desire for control is going to get them into some precarious situations. This is where parenting gets really hard. We are supposed to maintain some control of our children and to teach them boundaries and respect, but what about when they refuse to listen and they cross those boundaries and show a lack of respect? There are consequences, right? Consequences that we give them as their parents, and the natural consequences that come with sin. However, there's another set of consequences that we have a hard time facing—parental consequences. When our child does something wrong, we feel ashamed. We want to hide it, and sometimes, we even want to shield our kids from the natural consequences that follow, all because we don't want others to think less of us as parents. On the other hand, we want *everyone* to know when our child does something right. We plaster it all over social media. We put the bumper sticker on our car celebrating their honor roll. We find reasons to bring it up in conversation with other parents. We tell ourselves that we are simply celebrating our child's achievement, but really, we're just looking for a big pat on the back as a parent. Friends, I get both ends of this. I've been there, too. We want to be able to point to something our child has done so we can say, "See, I'm a good mom. I'm doing something right." And when our child has more trips to the principal's office than walks up on the stage to receive trophies and certificates, we feel like a failure. We feel embarrassed. Defeated. Out of control. And our kids feel it. They feel our complete disappointment and disapproval, which just perpetuates the cycle.

Sweet Mama, clenching control will steal your peace like nothing else will. The hard truth is that we will never know what's really around the corner for ourselves or our children. Life is messy and unpredictable. It's good to be prepared for anything and to assume the best, but striving for control is like trying to grab ahold of the wind. We convince ourselves that we have it in our grip, but it slides through our fingers the minute we think we have it. Total control is just an illusion, and God didn't design our hands or our hearts to hold it.

A prayer for the mom who struggles with control:

Dear Lord,

Help me to release my grip of control over my children and my life. I know it is based in fear and a lack of trusting You. Help me to trust You, Lord. I know You love my kids even more than I do. I place them in Your loving hands. Forgive me for trying to push my agenda over Your plan for my life and their lives, Lord. Thank You for Your patience with me as I learn how to trust You more, Lord.

In Jesus' name,
Amen

CHAPTER SEVEN

Excessive Expectations

Key Principle: Unmet and/or unrealistic expectations are difficult peace pirates, but we can manage our expectations well when we align them with God's expectations for our lives and homes.

"I feel underappreciated. I gave up everything I worked for to care for my family, and sometimes I feel like it doesn't matter. It's not that I need constant praise and adoration for this, but it would be nice to hear occasionally that what I'm doing is important work."

—Erin D., married mom of two

My two youngest sons and I love having lunch at Chick-fil-A because of the family-friendly atmosphere and delicious fast food—not to mention the amazing little play area. It's one of the few places where a little squeal by a toddler isn't taboo or frowned upon. A few years ago—as my then toddler and baby were simultaneously eating, squirming, and squealing with delight—I could feel a nearby older couple staring me down in judgment . . . or so I thought.

It was only around eleven o'clock, so the rambunctious, kid-heavy lunch crowd hadn't shown up yet. I realized that my two little munchkins probably appeared a little too loud. I felt the couple's eyes burning a hole through my back as my son flailed himself on the booth cushion and yelled out some silly statement due to his excitement awaiting little friends who might come to play with him. I shushed him and turned around to see if they were still staring at me. They quickly shifted their focus back to each other.

I started to give my then one-year-old some pieces of my chicken wrap. I thought I heard them gasp as I used my hands, instead of a fork or knife, and placed the food on the naked table, instead of on a plate or placemat. I heard them whispering about how gross it was. That *had* to be what they were talking about, right? *Why am I such a spectacle?* I thought to myself. *Have they never been around young children? I mean, this is a relatively uneventful, peaceful lunch in my book. Sheesh! Please, for the love, stop staring at me!*

I considered packing it all up and heading to the playground right then, but the baby started fussing a little. He was still hungry. So I reached into the diaper bag and took out his bottle of water and toddler formula. I attempted to unscrew the top of the bottle, but for some unknown reason, it just wouldn't budge. I started twisting it in various ways to get it to loosen. Nothing. Then the baby started to cry because he *saw* the bottle, and I was unable to give it to him right at that moment. The couple's stares began to feel more ominous than before—like lasers piercing through my back.

As my thoughts about their motives began to escalate, I could feel sweat on my upper lip. My body temperature began to rise, and I decided that we might want to cut our Chick-fil-A experience a little short today. I didn't want to deal with their judgment. Even so, my young brood and I had lasted this long, and I wanted to have a special time with my littles. So I decided to persist. I started pulling at the bottle top like a bodybuilder wannabe, but *still* it wouldn't budge.

Meanwhile, my toddler exclaimed to everyone in the restaurant that he wanted his "coffee." Once again, I felt the couple's persistent stares, and I, rather loudly, told my son that his "coffee" isn't actually called "coffee." "It's *creamer*, sweetie. You like to have *creamer*, and you can have *one* creamer as soon as you eat your nuggets," I said while laughing rather nervously and placing the bottle between my knees to try and get more of a grip on the top. By that point, I was sure the couple had written me off as a bad mom with loud kids, gross food-hygiene habits, and terrible grip strength. That was until they walked right over to me and the husband kindly asked, "Can I help you get that top off your bottle?"

I was shocked. The kindness and compassion in their eyes were overwhelming. I quickly said, "Yes! Please! I must have been too forceful when I put the top on before I left the house." When I tried to hand it to the kind older man, the top fell off *on its own*. Go figure! I thanked them, and his wife gave me a warm smile—the kind of smile that says, *I've been there, too, honey*, or *Don't worry! You're doing a great job, Mama*. Then they told me how precious my kids were, said good-bye, cleared their table, and left.

As I watched that sweet couple exit the restaurant, I felt so guilty for my snap judgment. I had assumed the worst of them and their motives, and I was sure they had the same kind of negative assumptions about me. They stared at me because they related to me, not because they were revolted by me or my kids. The wife's eyes wandered our way because she remembered how stressful things were when she was trying to manage two little ones by herself at a restaurant. The husband couldn't look away when I was fighting with the bottle top, because he remembered what a juggling act it can be to feed and calm two young kiddos. They just wanted to help. They noticed my struggle, and they were willing to lend a hand. I will never forget their kindness and that woman's reassuring and encouraging smile.

God taught me an important lesson through that couple: Our assumptions about people shape the expectations we have for them. We have the power to choose to see the best in people just as God chooses to see the best in us. When tensions rise, we tend to assume the worst about the people around us, and this only produces more anger, irritability, and negativity in us. Our perspective becomes skewed as well as our expectations. Ecclesiastes 10:13–14 states, "Fools base their thoughts on foolish assumptions, so their conclusions will be wicked madness; they chatter on and on" (NLT).

Man, that sums it right up, doesn't it? Though I don't like admitting it, I have been a foolish mother at times. I've felt what it's like to live in "wicked madness"—which is the perfect way to describe being under the rule of chaos, don't you think? As we discussed earlier in this book, our thoughts shape our actions. Ecclesiastes 10:13 teaches us that our "foolish assumptions" lead to certain "conclusions"—or expectations—that erode our peace and perspective. These expectations, usually left unspoken, are unrealistic. And when our loved ones don't meet them, we lose our temper and lash out. The peace pirate of unbridled, out-of-control expectations snickers in his triumph. Man, does this one get on my last nerve! This peace pirate is so stinkin' sneaky. And when I fall for his shenanigans, I become a raving lunatic to the ones I love most.

Can you relate? Do you feel like you are a ticking time bomb with your kids some days? When my youngest was still an infant, my day would go something like this: I would wake up in the morning to the sound of my two older boys fighting. In a tired stupor, I'd tell the boys to "get along," and make a beeline for the coffeepot. Meanwhile, my toddler would start screaming somewhere in the house. I'd run toward the sound, still half-awake, only to find that he'd fallen down and bumped his head for the thirty-sixth time after climbing on that thing that I'd asked him for the sixty-fifth time *not* to climb on. I'd kiss his boo-boo and then scold him for not listening yet again. Then I'd make my way back downstairs, only to see my two older boys fighting again. I'd send each of them to their room when I'd realize we had only ten minutes to get ready for school. Both boys would still be shirtless with horrific breath and crazy hair. So the punishment of sending them to their bedroom was a dud. *Sigh. Grumble.*

I'd tell myself to shake it off and focus. We'd scramble to get dressed, brush teeth, and look semi-presentable for school. Then, we'd say a quick prayer, and out the door they'd go. As I closed the door and backed up a little, I would bump into my sweet husband...who I hadn't even said hello to yet because I was so wrapped up in the kids and their shenanigans. We'd embrace for a few seconds, until the baby started crying. So my husband would make a bottle and then head out the door. I'd sit down to feed the baby just when my toddler would become hysterical because he couldn't find his Ninja Turtle. *Where is that Ninja Turtle?* I'd hold the baby and his bottle in his mouth in one arm while searching for the beloved lost toy with the other. Of course, I couldn't find it. I'd try to give my toddler another toy, but that just wouldn't cut it.

I'd put the baby down, and search for my coffee. When I finally found it, it was cold. *Boo.* I'd head to the pantry to find something to eat and realize that the kids had eaten every bit of the one thing I wanted that morning. *Boo again.* Then, my exhausted brain would start ticking and eventually...*Kaboom.* Enter "crazy mom." *I've had it! I just want a moment of silence!* I'd pace the floor. My toddler would try to talk to me, but I'd become so frustrated and angry that it all sounded like the teacher from *Charlie Brown*: *Wah, wah, wah.* Nobody in this house was rising to my expectations. They were all blowing it, and I was fed up! My peace and patience were nowhere to be found. I would escape to my bedroom and plop down on the bed. Mad. Disappointed. Defeated. Depleted. Then, I'd feel guilty for even *wanting* a moment of silence, and the shame would set in with accusing self-talk like: *What kind of mother tries to get away from her kids? Well, apparently, you do! You are blessed to have kids, and the fact that you sometimes just want to escape to a quiet, kid-less room is just terrible! You must be missing the mark if you feel the need to retreat. Shame on you, Mama. Shame on you!*

However, before I could fully give in to wallowing in my own pity and shame, the Holy Spirit would bring me back to reality and remind me of something essential that I had forgotten to do that morning—I hadn't taken a moment to connect with my Savior. At first, I would resist His loving and timely reminder, but as I reflected on all that had transpired that morning, I would realize that He was right, as He always is. I had approached the day without getting my mind and heart in the right place *first*.

How can I expect to approach my kids in a peaceful manner if I don't allow myself the opportunity to start the day in prayer—the primary way I can pursue, promote, and protect the peace in my heart and home?

Sometimes, I think I put too much stock in coffee. Truth

be told, I am not sure I could survive some mornings without it. But coffee can't bring me peace. It just boosts my energy for a moment and then sends me crashing down. Only God can give me the sustaining strength and peace I need to face the day. Friends, I don't know about you, but I desperately need His supernatural strength and perfect peace that surpasses my understanding. As I mentioned earlier, I absolutely love how Mark 4:39 describes the moment when Jesus calmed the chaotic ocean waves surrounding the disciples in their boat. It says, "Then he arose and rebuked the wind, and said to the sea, 'Peace, be still!' And the wind ceased and there was a great calm" (NKJV).

That's our Savior! He can calm the ocean waves with three commanding words; He can most definitely calm my heart before I even approach what lies ahead of me. I want to start my day with the only One who has the power to help me overcome complete chaos with peace and stillness. Don't you? All we need to do is commune with Him in prayer—a quiet moment where it's just your Savior and you having a conversation. A moment of stillness. A time to pursue His peace. Then, and only then, can we approach the day with the right perspective and healthy expectations.

Starting our day in prayer gives us time with our Savior—time to reflect and time to replenish our soul. Friend, we can't consider this quiet moment in the morning to be an afterthought or something we will "get to if time allows." We *need* this . . . for our sake *and* the sake of our families. A moment with God in the morning will give us peace and position us to boldly face the day.

We need strength to face our bountifully blessed but often hectic days. We need peace to navigate sibling fights, children who won't put on their "listening ears," teenagers full of angst, forgotten homework assignments, parent-teacher conferences, work deadlines, and a to-do list that seems to grow exponentially every day. We need a kid-free, silent moment *alone* to refuel and reconnect with our Savior *before* we utter a word to our kiddos.

I realize that many days this seems nearly impossible because we have some early risers or kids who end up in bed with us, but we *must* find a way. If we are going to stand against the pesky peace pirate of excessive expectations, then we must make morning prayer/quiet time a priority and be intentional with our time. Our peace and the peace within our home depend on it!

So what would it take? How can you make morning prayer a part of your daily routine? It may mean waking up earlier, making it a habit to say a quick prayer before exiting your bed, asking your husband to take on certain morning tasks, or having older kids help out more in the morning. If none of those things are possible, maybe shuffling the morning routine will help. One year, I purchased age-appropriate devotionals for each of our boys in an effort to encourage them to develop a habit of having their morning quiet time and to give me some much-needed quiet time with the Lord as well. It was a refreshing change that we kept for months. Over time, the younger kids became frustrated with the devotional time, and this caused the older boys to be distracted and frustrated as well. The whole point of this exercise was to promote peace, so we decided to switch things up again. Parenting is all about being willing to monitor and adjust as needed. Nowadays, we do a family devotional at the dinner table most nights, and we allow the kids to read or watch a short program in the morning while Dave and I have our moment with the Lord. The bottom line is that we *can* make a way. We must be proactive and assertive about this. Our family needs us to be at our best, and it will do our hearts good as well. Let's *do this*! Gone are the topsy-turvy days of crazy mommy moments in the morning and awful mommy guilt trips afterward. Yes, we will still make mistakes, but we will be in a much better state of mind and heart to weather the storms when they come.

I don't want to be a foolish mother, and I know you don't want to be a foolish mother, either. We want to be prayerful, positive, and peace-filled mamas who face each day with healthy expectations and do our best to love our families and serve the Lord. Are you with me?

So we know that starting our day with prayer will help us to pursue and promote peace in our hearts and homes, but what do we do when our expectations and the expectations others have for us run amuck? First, we must understand how to form healthy expectations. Proverbs 11:23 says, "The desire of the righteous ends only in good, the expectation of the wicked in wrath" (ESV). When I read this verse, I find it so interesting that the author, King Solomon, links "desire," or the feeling of *wanting something* to occur, with the "righteous," or those seeking the Lord. And he links "expectation," or a belief that *something should happen* or be a particular way, with "the wicked," or those not following the Lord who often only think of themselves. Isn't that fascinating? I don't think Solomon is trying to say that having any kind of expectation is inherently a bad thing. Clearly, he is teaching us that righteous motives and actions will ultimately lead to good things, and wicked motives and actions will lead to bad things. However, I think we need to pay close attention to his word choice here. When we *desire*, or want, our family member to do something, the actions we take to present that desire to them are much more tender in nature. On the other hand, when we *expect*, or think our family member should do this or that, it often comes from a place of assumption, which as we discussed before, often leads to great disappointment and misunderstanding.

Does this mean that we should never have any expectations for our kids or spouse? Absolutely not! However, it does mean that we might need to examine the expectations that we have a little more closely to see if a righteous desire is at the heart of them. For example, most of us want our kids to do well in school, so we have certain expectations when it comes to them getting good grades and favorable behavior marks. Every family is different, but most set specific standards when it comes to school. We have the expectation for our kids to make A/B honor roll, and when they get it, we reward their hard work with a trip to our local Froyo shop. Not all of my kids make A/B honor roll every time. They are all so gifted in their own way, but some are better students than others.

My son Connor is super smart and creative, but he doesn't consistently bring home grades that reflect his intellect. This used to really bother me, and I thought it was because I was disappointed in my son for not putting forth his best effort—that was until a few years ago. When it came time for the academic awards at the end of his fifth-grade year, Connor got invited. I couldn't believe it! He had made the A/B honor roll for only one quarter of the school year, so I thought that maybe he was going to be recognized for amazing behavior or excelling in a certain subject. Regardless, I was so proud of him and completely elated at the thought of seeing him up on that stage.

When I attended the awards ceremony, a lot of my friends were there with their kids. We were all so excited that our kids were going to be recognized. To be honest, I kind of felt extra-special to be a part of this group. My mama pride was raging that day. Then came the ceremony. They recognized the best of the best in every subject, gave character and service awards, and then, at the very end, they recognized kids who had participated in completing a special project. That's when my son finally got to go to the stage and be recognized. My heart sank. He was basically being recognized for participating in something that his teacher had required them to do. I think he received a printed-out certificate, when all the other kids, who received academic awards of excellence, were given medals.

I'm sad to say that I was totally embarrassed and even a little angry. I mean, what a waste of time, right? What a way to bring a kid's (and a mother's) hopes up! I was prepared for my son to be completely devastated and embarrassed, too, but he wasn't. When I came down the aisle to greet him along with all the other parents hugging their kids with multiple medals hanging around their necks, my son was smiling from ear to ear. The first thing he said to me was, "Isn't that so cool that Claire got the character award for the whole grade? I even got a picture of her on stage! I'm so glad I was here to see it." I hugged him, and boy, did I feel like a big phony. Goodness. There I was, embarrassed, having a full-on mommy pity party, while my son could not have cared less about his personal certificate or the fact that he didn't receive a medal. Connor was relishing some of his last moments as a fifth-grader, and he was truly happy for his dear friend. I realized what a fool I had been. My desire for my son to receive an award wasn't righteous in the least. It was selfish. I wanted to bask in his glory. I wanted other parents in the room to think I must be doing a good job because my son got the math award, or whatever. *Sheesh!* I'm embarrassed to admit that, but it's the truth.

When we don't have a righteous desire—an honorable and Godly reason—behind our expectations, they become "unbridled" to the One who gives us our peace. As one who grew up in Kentucky—the Horse Capital of the World—I've heard the term "unbridled" used quite a bit. A "bridle" is the head contraption that is placed on a horse in order to lead and control it. It is the very thing that allows a person to keep the horse focused on where it needs to go. So when a horse is "unbridled," it is uncontrolled, unrestrained, and uncontained, and it can end up causing harm to itself and those around it. I don't know if you

have ever seen a horse come out of the safety of its bridle, but it is a scary sight. It runs around aimlessly at a high
speed, bucking its back legs, and throwing up its front legs.
The horse is frustrated and doesn't quite know what to do
or where to go. Friends, this is how we often react when
our expectations become unbridled. However, the bridle
in this case is on our hearts. Just as the horse chooses to
surrender to its bridle and the person leading it, we must
choose to surrender our hearts to the Lord's bridle and
trust Him to lead us where we need to go. He is the One
who helps us to cultivate a righteous desire that leads to
healthy expectations, and the Holy Spirit helps us to discern when our desire isn't Godly and is selfish in nature.

The more we seek the Lord and surrender to Him,
the more our desires and eventual expectations will fall in
line with His will. And peace will follow. During Jesus'
Sermon on the Mount, He says, "Seek the Kingdom of
God above all else, and live righteously, and he will give
you everything you need" (Matt. 6:33 NLT). I have read
this verse so many times as well as heard it preached in
sermons, but when I look at it through the lens of expectations, it takes on a whole new meaning. You see, there is
big difference between seeking and expecting. The Google
Dictionary defines "seek" as to "attempt or desire to ob-
tain or achieve something" and to "ask for (something)
from someone." However, the definition of "expect" is
to "look for (something) from someone as rightfully due
or requisite in the circumstances" and to "require (someone) to fulfill an obligation." Do you see the difference?
When we seek the Lord, we are following a righteous de-

sire to connect with Him and pursue His will. Whereas when we place our expectations on God (or anyone else for that matter), we are often driven by our own selfish desires to get what we believe we are owed. Seeking is asking; expecting is a passive-aggressive demand. Again, it is not inherently wrong to expect God to fulfill His promises as written in the Word or to have certain expectations for our kids, spouse, and even ourselves, but it is better to ask, and not demand, for those things in the most loving way possible.

One of my favorite verses is Matthew 7:7 when Jesus says, "Keep on asking, and you will receive what you ask for. Keep on seeking, and you will find. Keep on knocking, and the door will be opened to you" (NLT). God wants to give us the desires of our heart, but He is a righteous God and will only fulfill righteous desires. So what unrighteous desires have led you to form excessive expectations for your family and yourself? What subject or situation seems to always form you into a ticking time bomb mom? Think about the root of the disappointment and frustration, and hand it over to God. Ask Him to give you righteous desires and healthy expectations, and He will. He will renew your mind and replace false beliefs and selfish desires with His truth and will for your life (Rom. 12:2 and Phil. 4:8).

Forming healthy expectations for our family and ourselves will go a long way in pursuing, promoting, and protecting the peace in our hearts and homes, but how do we make those expectations known? It all comes down to calm, clear, consistent, and caring communication. One of the biggest mistakes I made with this early on was expecting—there's that word again—my family to read my mind and body language without me actually telling them what I needed. I would huff and puff, stomp, grimace, and eye roll my way through it, and man, did that let the excessive expectation peace pirate get a foothold in our home. I never received the response I was hoping for. Go figure! Instead of "Yes, ma'am," my kids would argue and complain, which would send me over the edge and onto the plank. Before I even realized I was doing it, I would lash out sharply at them, call them lazy and disrespectful, and end up stomping away, only to feel guilt and shame. The Holy Spirit would convict me, and I would apologize for my reaction, but then, I would often fall back into the same negative cycle. That was until I realized that I was going about it all wrong. I should have asked my kids and husband for what I needed in a calm, clear, consistent, and caring way from the start. For my children, this meant writing it on a board and posting it somewhere they could see it daily as a reminder. I would use pictures and symbols for the younger kids who weren't reading yet. Over the years, we've tweaked this system as needed, but it has helped us communicate what we need them to do as part of this family, and it has promoted and protected the peace in our home.

A few years ago, my husband and I were totally at odds with our kids. Day after day, we would be getting everyone ready for bed and see that the two older boys, then ages eight and ten, had been careless with their chores. This had become a terrible cycle.

You might be familiar with it, too...

Mom and Dad tell kids to do "X, Y, and Z" chores by "such-and-such" time.

Kids begin the chores and try to finish them...carelessly...as fast as they can.

Mom and Dad tell kids to go back and do them AGAIN.

They do...well, sort of. Things are still messy, and bad attitudes begin to erupt from both kids and parents.

Mom and Dad get angry, scold the kids, and have the kids do their chores YET AGAIN...or the parents end up doing the work themselves because they are exhausted from this song and dance.

Ever been there? Well, that is exactly where we were. Furious. Exhausted. Disappointed. I felt like I was at the point of fracturing my relationship with our kids because it seemed to always end in an argument...something I said I would *never* do with my kids. Right? I can faintly hear my pre-mom self declaring, "I will never engage in an argument with *my* kids!" *Ugh.* Failed that one.

After dealing with this for too long, I decided to try something new (at least to us). It's not earth-shattering or complicated in any way, but it has completely changed the way my kids, and even I, see household chores. I decided to designate a "Chore Day" where the *whole* family cleans the *whole* house at the same time.

Since Saturday has become our Sabbath, or rest day, I decided to make ours Sunday morning before we went to church. We wake up, have breakfast, and assign tasks. As I mentioned before, my reading kids respond well to having things clearly written down. They enjoy checking each item off the list. For the last few years, we've had Cooper, our eldest, vacuum upstairs, Swiffer-mop the bathroom upstairs and downstairs, wipe the baseboards downstairs, empty the dishwasher, put away his laundry, and clean his room. We have Connor, our second eldest, who is now eleven, dust the furniture, clean the upstairs bathroom, wipe the baseboards upstairs, load the dishwasher, put away his laundry, and clean his room. Chandler, who is currently seven, has "air freshener duty" upstairs, puts away his clothes, wipes the bathroom counter upstairs, and cleans his room. Our youngest, Chatham, who is four, picks up his toys, makes his toddler bed, and makes sure our little dog, Chi Chi, is outside when the vacuuming starts. My husband does the laundry, changes lightbulbs, mows the lawn, and landscapes...which is some amazing "chore play," if you know what I mean (*wink, wink*). I mop the kitchen and hardwoods downstairs, vacuum the downstairs rugs and bedroom, clean the master bedroom and bathroom, completely scrub the kitchen, put clean sheets on the bed, and start the dishwasher. As I am finishing up my chores, the older two boys rotate being on "Chatham Duty," or making sure our youngest doesn't get lost in the shuffle.

When we're all working together, the relative silence is like music to my ears. We are all doing our part to maintain our home. This doesn't negate daily chores like putting away clothes and tidying up bedrooms, but Chore Day has made a huge difference in all of our attitudes. Here's why I think it works:

1. The kids are "helping with" and "responsible for" certain cleaning tasks. We are sure to use those key words when having our kids do their chores because it changes their perspective. They respond much better to, "Can you help me with _____?" as opposed to, "Go clean _____." I also try to praise their work whenever I can. It's neat to see them beaming over a job well done.

2. The kids realize how much work goes into taking care of a home. Ever since we instituted Chore Day, the kids have been even more willing to pitch in throughout the week. They have a better understanding of how long it takes to do laundry and clean all these rooms because they are doing the job. There's no better teacher than that of experience.

3. The kids are learning real-life skills. I often tell my boys that Chore Day is preparing them to be better husbands and fathers. They laugh it off and shake their heads, but I honestly believe it. Our kids need to know how to take care of themselves and others. As they clean, I am sure to thank them for helping take care of our home. When they keep an eye on their baby brother as I finish mopping, I am sure to praise them for taking care of him. I want my boys to understand these essential life skills, and Chore Day is full of those teachable moments.

4. The kids aren't focused on themselves—they are focused on the task at hand and helping the family. As kids, we start out thinking that the world revolves around us. We go from one fun thing to another. Yes, kids need to have lots of time to play and explore, but it is so important for us to teach our kids that life is not all about them. In fact, it's not all about us, the parents, either. It's about loving God, loving others, and serving the world. Chore Day helps to instill these values on a very basic and simple level.

5. Mom and Dad don't feel as overwhelmed with household tasks because the kids are pitching in. Ever since we started Chore Day, I haven't felt as overwhelmed. It's so nice to have the kids help. I often felt at odds with them when they wouldn't live up to my expectations in doing their chores. Now that we are all working together on Chore Day, there is more peace in our home.

If you are reading this and think Chore Day might be something that could bring more peace to your family, it's important to consider the following: First, make sure that your cleaning products are safe for kids. I've learned that "natural" doesn't necessarily mean it's safe for kids, so be sure to do your research. Second, remember that the assigned chores for each child need to be age-appropriate. Can they reach the area you want them to clean? Can they understand your directions as to how to complete the chore? Are they physically able to complete the task? Third, it's important to be consistent with Chore Day. Try to implement it at the same time every week. Then, it will become part of your weekly routine. Fourth, tie the successful completion of their assigned chores to a specific reward. For example, our kids receive their weekly allowance based on fully completing their chores and having good attitudes/behavior throughout the week. Fifth, don't give up if it doesn't go perfectly! This is one I have to remind myself of *every* Chore Day. As long as the area gets cleaned, clothes and dishes are put away, and everything is tidy, then I need to be thankful. The kids may not do a specific chore *exactly* the way I would, but I choose to be happy as long as the job is done well. The kids are learning, so we need to give them some grace as they get better at completing each chore. Finally, and most important, make it fun! Turn on some music. Have some cookies waiting for when you all finish your chores. Dance while you are cleaning. Be silly! Believe it or not, Chore Day can offer up some quality family time that you just might enjoy!

When Excessive Expectations Are Placed on You

One of the trickiest schemes that the peace pirate of excessive expectations tries to pull off is convincing us that we need to make everyone happy. I've struggled with this one for years, and the older I get and the closer I walk with the Lord, the more I realize that this cannot and should not be my aim. People are fickle—even our loved ones. As human beings, we are prone to changing our minds, giving our feelings too much stock in our decision making, and looking to others for validation. Friends, this will only perpetuate relationship problems and erode our peace. So how do we fight against this? We strive to be peacemakers. Matthew 5:9 records Jesus as declaring, "Blessed are the peacemakers, for they will be called children of God."

I love that, don't you? The more we strive to be at peace with God, ourselves, and others, the more we live like Christ. However, this is not stating that we must strive to make everyone happy. There is a huge difference. Sometimes, we must address a hard truth in a loving way, but the person on the receiving end may not like it. Sometimes, we have to establish healthy boundaries with ourselves and an extended family member in order to keep the peace in our home, and that won't necessarily make that extended family member happy. We aren't called to pacify those who are stronger willed than us. We are called to love them, and when you truly love someone, you tell them the truth in love—not by screaming it in their face, or instigating a fight, or giving them the cold shoulder when they don't listen to you. We love them by always striving to pursue a peaceful relationship with them but also refusing to be their doormat. In Romans 12:18, the apostle Paul writes, "If it is possible, as far as it depends on you, live at peace with everyone."

I think that one statement sums up being a peacemaker more than any other verse because it addresses the fact that some people make it impossible for you to live at peace with them—and that is between that person and the Lord. We can't fix everything, and we can't expect to be able to make everyone like us. There are times when our children won't like the appropriate consequences that we give them, but this doesn't mean we throw the consequences out the window so our kids will be happy with us once again. That would only make things worse. We would become a doormat, and our kids would morph into master manipulators who never truly understand the difference between right and wrong. Instead, we must stand up for truth and justice in the most loving way possible and remind them that God's love for us and our love for them have nothing to do with what they do or don't do or the fact that they got in trouble. We actively protect the peace in our hearts and homes when we make it our mission to be peacemakers while also refusing to become somebody's doormat both inside and outside our home. This means we calmly yet clearly tell our husband when his words and tone hurt us. We sit our kids down, look them in the eye, and tell them that they can't slam the door in our face when they're mad. We tell them there are healthier ways to handle anger like going for a run, journaling, listening to music, or even screaming into a pillow. It also means saying "No" to some "good" things that we just don't have the time and energy to do. Yes, this may disappoint our friend or coworker, but we won't have peace and be at our best when we are running ourselves ragged trying to make everybody happy with us. This is especially difficult for people like me who tend to be "people-pleasers" or perfectionists about certain things. However, this only distracts us from God's will, defeats our spirit, and depletes our energy. We ultimately end up having pent-up anger and resentment because we feel used.

When You Place Unrealistic Expectations on Yourself

Friend, anger isn't inherently bad; it's how we handle it that gets us in trouble. This is something I need to remind myself often, because sometimes, I'm the one who puts unrealistic expectations on myself. Then, when everything falls apart, I get angry and frustrated, and instead of handling it in a healthy way, I'm snippy with the ones I love most, stomping around the house like a toddler having a temper tantrum. Sound familiar? We often hold ourselves to a standard that we would never put on anyone else—especially when it comes to motherhood. We try to be and do everything for everybody. But truth is, we simply cannot do it all. God certainly doesn't expect us to do it all, and His desire for our lives is the most important one of all.

So how can we rein in our own expectations and protect the peace in our heart and home? A good exercise is to do these three things: Write down the expectations you have for yourself; then look at each expectation and write down the desire that is at the heart of each expectation; and finally, write down how each expectation promotes peace in your heart and home. If the desire isn't a righteous—or holy—one, then you need to adjust your "why" behind that expectation or take that expectation off the list. If it doesn't bring your heart and home more peace, then it probably doesn't belong on your list in this season. It's also important to consider whether or not your expectations are realistic. Ask yourself, "Is this expectation something I can feasibly do in this season?" If the answer is "No," then it would be wise to shelve it and reconsider it in another season when there is less on the schedule.

Let's work through one example of how to do this exercise. Let's say one of my expectations is to organize every classroom party for all four of my sons this school year. That would be equal to about sixteen parties. When I think about my desire, or reason, for wanting to do this, my first answer would probably be, "I just want to be present for those moments with my kids." But when I look further into my reason for wanting to be *in charge* of planning the parties, my real desire is to prove what a creative, crafty, and amazing mom I can be. *Sigh.* So I think about how to rework this expectation in such a way to bring more peace to myself and my family. I decide that attending the parties would fulfill my righteous desire to be present for special moments with my kids. I also decide to plan one or two parties this school year to fulfill the righteous desire to help out at school. Now my expectation is one that will help to pursue, promote, and protect the peace in my heart and home.

I remind myself that if I can't attend all sixteen or so parties or even plan those one or two parties, I am not a failure. I will do the best I can and know that these expectations do not define my value as a mother. God loves me, my husband, and my kids more than I ever could, and He is with me every step of the way—equipping me, comforting me, cheering me on, redirecting me, and restoring me. Thank You, Lord!

Friend, God is doing the very same thing for you. He longs to hear your voice every day. He wants you to know Him more and more, and He doesn't want the peace pirate of excessive expectations to throw you for a loop. God is the God of Peace, and He wants to bring you and your family peace today and every day.

A prayer for those who are struggling with excessive expectations:

Dear Lord,

Thank You for loving us. Help us to focus our mind and heart on You and all that You desire from us. You tell us that Your yoke is easy and Your burden is light. May we shake off any unrealistic expectations that we are placing on ourselves or on our loved ones. Help us to cultivate healthy expectations fueled by a righteous desire to live a life that is pleasing to You—a life that is filled with peace and leads to Jesus.

In Jesus' name,

Amen

Peace Pirate Assessment

Now that you have learned about the four peace pirates, I encourage you to take the following assessment to help you determine your primary and secondary peace pirates. Please keep in mind that whichever peace pirate(s) you might be vulnerable to has a lot to do with your season of life and the age of your children. This is an assessment that will be beneficial to take more than once to get a better gauge of what might be plundering your peace. So here goes! Pick one answer that describes your most likely (or first) response to each of the following scenarios:

1. When I get a call that my child misbehaved at daycare/ school, my first thought is:
   A. I'm not doing enough to teach him/her right from wrong. This is on me.
   B. Why can't my child be more like Cindy's kid? He/she is so well behaved.
   C. I have done everything in my power to teach him/her how to behave. This is an outrage!
   D. Why isn't my child filling up his/her good be- havior chart instead of getting in trouble? I am so disappointed and embarrassed.

2. My child's teacher personally asks me to be a chap- erone on an important school field trip, but I have a scheduling conflict. I respond by:
   A. Doing whatever it takes to attend both events, even if it makes for a crazy busy day.
   B. Asking what other moms are going and who went on the last field trip to see if it's really worth changing my schedule and making an ap- pearance.
   C. Asking the teacher if he/she might consider do- ing the field trip on another day or at another time of day so, ultimately, I can attend.
   D. Feeling stressed that the teacher asked me to vol- unteer and that I might not be able to grant his/ her request and also let my child down.

3. I scroll through Facebook and see that my friend's son became "Student of the Month" for the second time

this year, but my child hasn't received this award yet. My first thought is:

A. That's awesome. She must be better at helping him with his projects than I am. I need to do a better job.

B. For the second time? Mine rarely if ever gets student of the month. Good for him... and her. *Sigh*.

C. I have asked the teachers what it takes to get Student of the Month, and we—my child and I—have strategically done these things with excellence. What's the deal?

D. This teacher must not like my child or notice anything good that he/she does.

4. The laundry pile is growing larger by the day at my house, so I:

A. Stay up way past my normal bedtime after a busy day and don't ask any family members for help.

B. Do a small portion of the pile just so it doesn't look messy or ridiculous if a friend decides to drop by unannounced.

C. Use this opportunity to give my kids a lesson on how to properly wash and fold clothes and make a schedule for when they will each do the laundry that week.

D. Lecture the kids and my spouse for the laundry getting so bad because they should've seen the pile and pitched in.

5. I am already running late and now traffic is backed up. It looks like my child and I are going to miss the basketball banquet, so I:

   A. Frantically get on every traffic and GPS app I have and scour them for an alternate route. I can't miss this!

   B. Call the coach to see if my child might be getting a special award or not to decide whether it might be worth showing up late, if at all.

   C. Call the coach and a few other parents to see if they, too, might be running late and try to convince them to change the start time.

   D. Feel frustrated with myself that I didn't leave earlier. Traffic is usually not that bad this time of night.

6. My child is voted "Most Likely to Succeed" at school, so I:

   A. Count it as a win for my child *and* for me, because I know that I got my child to where they are through my sacrifice.

   B. Congratulate my child and also ask him/her what other awards/superlatives were given and who received them.

   C. Take a pic of my child with his/her certificate and post it on all my social media channels to congratulate my child and bring attention to his/her other accolades.

   D. Am ecstatic because that was the exact award/superlative I thought he/she would receive.

7. My eight-year-old niece accepts Jesus and gets baptized at church. My ten-year-old child hasn't been baptized yet, so I:

   A. Attend my niece's baptism and celebrate her, while also deciding to read the Bible more to my child. I assume that's why he hasn't accepted Jesus yet.

   B. Ask my friends if their kids are baptized yet to get a gauge of when most kids accept Christ, to decide if I should be concerned.

   C. Decide to enter my child in the "Growing Your Faith" class at church and pray that he/she gets baptized at the end of the six weeks.

   D. Don't worry about it because I got baptized at twelve.

You've completed the assessment! Now, count how many A's, B's, C's, and D's you have.

   Number of A's =
   Number of B's =
   Number of C's =
   Number of D's =

If your highest number of answers were A's, then your primary peace pirate is Mommy Martyrdom. If your highest number of answers were B's, then you are prone to struggling with the Comparison Chaos peace pirate. If your highest number of answers were C's, then you probably have issues with the Clenching Control peace pirate. If your highest number of answers were D's, then the Excessive Expectation peace pirate causes you difficulty. Now, look at your second-highest number, and consider what your secondary peace pirate might be. If you have a fairly even split among all the letters, no worries! This just means that you might struggle with all the peace pirates to some degree and possibly in specific circumstances.

Sweet Mama, please remember that this assessment is not definitive and can change based on the season of parenting you are in. This assessment is simply a tool to help you understand more about yourself and your level of vulnerability to each peace pirate. It might even help to read the four peace pirate chapters again after finding out your results. Be sure to pay close attention to how you can fight your primary and secondary peace pirates in each of those chapters, and you will be on your way to having more of God's peace in your heart and home.

PART III

Treasure Up

"*I have two beautiful, rambunctious boys who are full of energy and always seem to 'need' me. Even though it can be frustrating, I do try to remind myself to treasure this time. Someday they won't 'need' me the same way, and I know that I will miss those times. I have to continuously remind myself of this especially when my kids keep me up at night because they 'need' mommy.*"

—Angela C., married mom of two

CHAPTER EIGHT

Mary, Imperfect and Faithful

Key Principle: Mary, the mother to the Savior of the World, didn't strive to measure up; instead, she chose to be faithful and "treasure up" the perfectly imperfect blessings right in front of her. We can choose to do this, too.

Throughout the last seven chapters, we've been on a journey to pursue, promote, and protect the peace in our hearts and homes. We've learned that God's peace isn't simply the absence of chaos—it's God pulling us out from under the authority of chaos and into His loving arms. It's us choosing to surrender to God and His authority, even when it feels like everything around us is falling apart. He holds us together. Only He can make us whole. We've also learned that we are in a spiritual battle for our peace. The enemy's peace pirates are on the prowl and out to plunder our peace in crafty ways. However, we've also learned how to identify each peace pirate's influence in our own lives and how to arm ourselves and our families against them. So what now? What else do we need to understand about peace? As I've prayed and pondered this question over the years, I can't help but think of Mary, the mother of Jesus.

I have always been fascinated by Mary and her story of tremendous faith, trust, and the most important parenting gig ever. I mean, I think I feel the daunting pressure from my calling as a parent to my boys, but can you imagine the pressure she must have felt trying to raise the Savior of the World? I get nervous just thinking about it. The amazing thing I've learned about Mary is that she found a way to rise above the pressure and focus on the blessings around her right in the moment—even the messiest and scariest moments of her life. In Luke 1:26–33, we learn how Mary first found out that she was going to parent the Savior of the World:

> God sent the angel Gabriel to Nazareth, a town in Galilee, to a virgin pledged to be married to a man named Joseph, a descendant of David. The virgin's name was Mary. The angel went to her and said, "Greetings, you who are highly favored! The Lord is with you."
> **Mary was greatly troubled at his words and wondered what kind of greeting this might be.** But the angel said to her, "Do not be afraid, Mary; you have found favor with God. You will conceive and give birth to a son, and you are to call him Je-

sus. He will be great and will be called the Son of the Most High. The Lord God will give him the throne of his father David, and he will reign over Jacob's descendants forever; his kingdom will never end.

Wow. Can you imagine an *angel* appearing to you and telling you this? I think I would just stand there with my mouth gaping open and my heart beating out of my chest. I'd be pinching myself to make sure I wasn't dreaming or hallucinating. I wouldn't know what to say or even how to react. I might have even tried to run away in fear, because the whole thing is kind of freaky, right?

Even though this happened over two thousand years ago, it's apparent that Mary was taken aback by Gabriel's appearance, to say the least. Go back and read the bolded words in the verses above. I put Mary's reactions and words in bold to show the relatable humanity in her responses. Friend, we often perceive Mary only as a perfectly peaceful statue without human feelings or frailties. We see her as Jesus' perfect mom and Joseph's perfect wife who never questioned God's plan for her life and never lost her temper. Some of us imagine her as always having a pleasant smile and prayer hands. Many of us have a little figurine of Mary as part of our Nativity scene that we display at Christmastime. We place her figurine on the table beside Baby Jesus, Joseph, the three wise men, an angel, the shepherds, and the animals. We admire it and celebrate the birth, as we should. Then, we put them all away with the rest of the Christmas décor for safekeeping until the next year. We don't consider her humanity or the reality of the

Nativity. However, when we hone in on those verses—when we ponder her reactions and responses as she is given the tall task to bring the greatest gift ever into the world—we see Mary as a young, inexperienced, afraid, innocent, imperfect, yet faithful woman. This is good news for the rest of us!

Mary wasn't perfect! She had natural human reactions to Gabriel's visit just like any of us would, and for good reason. In both the Old and the New Testaments, we learn that Gabriel appeared to be something like a man (Dan. 9:21), but when we read about others who also encountered Gabriel (Daniel and Zacharias), it's clear that he usually frightened people—not on purpose, of course. We know this because he always responded to their obvious fright by reassuring them and telling them not to be afraid. So I am sure Mary was troubled by Gabriel's man-like yet otherworldly presence just as much as she was shocked and even confused by the news he was revealing to her. She even questioned him saying, "How will this be . . . since I am a virgin?" (Luke 1:34). This is a valid question. Mary was engaged to Joseph and had kept her promise not to be physically intimate with her betrothed until they were married. Gabriel must've sensed her reluctance and very human need to try to understand how any of this would feasibly occur, because he went on to explain how God would make this seemingly impossible calling on her life possible and proved that God had already done the impossible with her cousin Elizabeth. In Luke 1:35–37, Gabriel told her, "The Holy Spirit will come on you, and the power of the Most High will overshadow you. So the holy one to be born will be called the Son of God. Even Elizabeth your relative is going to have a child in her old age, and she who was said to be unable to conceive is in her sixth month. For no word from God will ever fail."

Gabriel greeted Mary by acknowledging God's favor on her life and presence with her, but he also appealed to Mary's human need for some proof. She believed in the Lord with all her heart, but she still had questions about what the angel was telling her. Gabriel didn't respond negatively to her question by telling her to just deal with it or shame her for being curious or hesitant. He did his very best to explain God's plan and reassured her by using Elizabeth's example as proof that God keeps His promises. After Mary heard Gabriel's explanation and the news of Elizabeth's pregnancy, she must have perked right up. Elizabeth was her beloved cousin who had longed to conceive a child for years, to no avail, but like Mary, Elizabeth had tremendous faith. She kept praying. I'm sure she also asked Mary and other family members to pray—for years. So when Mary heard this amazing news of God fulfilling Elizabeth's lifelong desire to have a child, I bet her heart leapt out of her chest. She believed that Gabriel truly was a messenger from the Lord, and she accepted His amazing, yet weighty will for her life. In Luke 1:38, she responds to Gabriel in stating, "I am the Lord's servant. . . . May your word to me be fulfilled."

What trust and faith! Mary chose to faithfully believe, embrace, and complete the enormous tasks that God put before her. Even the ones she didn't fully understand. She knew that God was with her, and the very embodiment of

Peace was growing inside her. She didn't accept this mission blindly, though. Mary asked questions, and I bet she wrestled through a lot of things with the Lord. Becoming a mother can bring on more questions than answers, even when you're not carrying the Messiah in your womb. Motherhood, in general, is a high calling and comes with great responsibility. We feel it every day, and we question whether things in our home are "normal." Maybe you've considered questions like the following:

How can someone so small create such a mess?

The struggle is real. We clean. They mess. We have them clean up after themselves. They do...a little. And then more mess. Whew! Just talking about it is exhausting, and it's just part of raising little ones. If we turn our back for a moment, total chaos will ensue. And we all know it's the quiet moments that are the most dangerous.

What's that awful smell?

The smells that kids create are crazy! As a mom with four boys, I've smelled the nastiest "creations" from who knows where that my kids have made outside. There's lots of sweat, budding body odor issues, plenty of toilets left unflushed, and an endless supply of flatulence. Yeah, it's constantly a game of "name that smell" at our house. But it's just part of being a mom, right?

Is it nap time/bedtime yet?

As moms, we go strong all day long. And some days drag on like molasses. It's on those *long* and difficult days of correcting, redirecting, cleaning up, breaking up sibling fights, disciplining again, cleaning up again, running kids all around town, and so on that we long for nap time and bedtime. The kids even start to show signs of exhaustion, but they fight it with every fiber of their being. Then, our patience wears thin, because—for the love of sanity and peace—we just need a moment. Seriously, sometimes, nap time/bedtime just can't come fast enough.

Who can I get to babysit for us so we can sneak away for a much-needed date night?

For married moms, this is on our minds a *lot*. Sometimes, tending to our children leaves little time for us to invest in our marriages. But we know we need to make the time. There are times we have to move Heaven and earth to make it happen, but our persistence will see us through. And our marriage will be stronger for it.

When was the last time my kids had a bath or shower (because their hair smells like garbage)?

Shew! I've been asking this question a lot these days. Honestly, how does their hair get so stinky so fast? It truly baffles me. This question only gets more frequent as our kids get older because they are the ones in charge of cleaning their own bodies. And yet they still need reminders. Like every day.

What am I forgetting?

This question riddles my mind more than I'd like to admit. As moms, we are constantly on the go—both figuratively and literally—so there are times when things get jumbled up in our minds. We know we are forgetting something, but we just can't put our finger on it. So we stop and go through our mental list of to-dos to try to figure it out. Most of the time, we do. But sometimes we don't. And that's okay. As long as we don't forget our kiddos. (*Ahem.* More about this later.)

Can you relate? Maybe you have pondered these and other practical questions, but maybe you have deeper questions as well—ones that can keep you up at night. Questions like...

Do my kids know how much I love them, and have I shown love to them today?

Sometimes, we get busy. Frustrated. Exhausted. We get to the end of the day and wonder if our kids know how much we love them. So we go into their bedrooms and take a moment to watch them sleep, and we thank God for the great gift that they are to us. We kiss them on their foreheads and tell them how much we love them, and we decide that we will tell them again when they are awake. Every mom knows that she can never say it enough.

Am I teaching the kids how to show love, kindness, respect, honor, etc., to others?

As moms, this is our heart's desire. We want to help our kids to become loving, kind, respectful, respectable, and honorable people. And sometimes, we struggle to figure out how we can teach them this on a daily basis. We read books and blogs and try new approaches all the time, because we so desperately want our kids to become loving and kind citizens who pursue their purpose and make a difference in the world.

What if "X, Y, and Z" happen to the kids?

Anytime we hear tragic stories of terrible things happening to kids, fear invades our hearts and minds. We wonder, "What if _____ happened to my kids?" It's paralyzing, and sometimes, it even keeps us up at night. This fear stems from the tremendous love we have for our kids and the knowledge that we don't control their future. Stuff happens—really awful stuff. But the truth is, really awesome stuff happens, too. And as moms, we need to strive to keep our focus on the good.

How in the world are we going to make it through this phase?

I once polled some moms on my Facebook page and asked them which phase of child-rearing was the hardest. What I found was surprising. Before they answered this question, they also had to provide some information about the current ages of their kids. You know what I found out? Each mom who answered the survey claimed that the "newest" child-rearing phase they were in was the hardest. In other words, the phase that their eldest child was going through was the hardest because it was something they had never experienced before. Isn't that interesting? That tells me that every phase has its challenges—especially when we are experiencing it for the first time as parents.

Sweet Mama, I find comfort in that, don't you? Just like Mary, God truly never gives us more than we can handle with His help. He is right with us (and our kids) through each and every phase. Each season brings blessings and challenges, and it's okay to ask questions. However, we can't allow our questions to overshadow our peace. Remember, God's peace "surpasses understanding" and "guards and hearts and minds in Christ Jesus" (Phil. 4:7), so there are going to be some things on this side of Heaven that we will never understand. God doesn't want us to re-play these questions over and over in our minds, because that only exhausts and confuses us and allows the peace pirates to enter in. God is a God of order and peace (1 Cor.14:33), and we can keep our questions from over-shadowing our peace when we consciously choose to trust God and faithfully carry out the tasks He gives us one step at a time. This can seem nearly impossible when the stakes are high and we feel unequipped, but Mary's story of faith-fulness despite imperfection offers us hope and a blueprint for the peaceful path.

When it became known that Mary was pregnant out of wedlock, her husband, Joseph—a kind and honorable man—decided that he would end their engagement quietly (Matt. 1:19). I'm sure he was so hurt and convinced that

Mary had slept with another man, regardless of her plea that her child was conceived by the Holy Spirit. Like Mary, Joseph had so many questions, yet God didn't fault him for this. Instead, He wanted to bring peace to Joseph's heart and his relationship with Mary, so God sent Gabriel to Joseph in a dream and confirmed what Mary had told him. They married but did not consummate their marriage until Jesus was born so there would be no room for doubt that He was conceived by the Holy Spirit. Even so, the couple must have endured such hardship during those months before the birth. As far as we know, the townspeople didn't have angels appearing to them to change their assumptions that Mary had cheated on Joseph and become pregnant in the process. I'm sure there were whispers whenever they were out in public together. Some probably wrote Mary off as a harlot. Others looked at Joseph as a fool. In the midst of public shame and isolation, Mary and Joseph remained faithful and hopeful. It brings tears to my eyes when I think about it. I long for that kind of trust and faith regardless of naysayers and misunderstanding.

One could imagine that Mary—heavy with child, exhausted, walking as far as she could, riding a donkey as far as she could bear, desperately looking for a place to give birth, turned away time and time again, afraid of the unknown yet in great anticipation of her impending delivery—would have been too spent to even form a thought, but she didn't fold under pressure. Despite being young and inexperienced, she exhibited a kind of wisdom and faithfulness that I strive for as a mother. She didn't allow herself to be distracted by trying to create some socially acceptable standard for her labor and delivery. Mary and Joseph stayed the course and found the humblest and most undesirable place to give birth, because it was what God made available to them. It was all part of His plan. Mary gave birth to the Savior of the World—peace, hope, and love wrapped in flesh—on some hay, surrounded by animals on a cold, dark night. How beautiful Jesus' first cry must have been! I can only imagine that Mary must have experienced such a mixture of feelings in that moment. The relief of giving birth to a healthy baby. The overwhelming joy of seeing and holding God's gift to the world. The incredible weight of the responsibility to raise the Messiah. I am sure Mary had so many questions filling her mind, and she probably wasn't even sure how she should feel at that moment. Honestly, how could she? Her pregnancy and motherhood experience were unprecedented, but that didn't overwhelm her. Instead, she chose to remain faithful to God's call on her life and "treasure up" His goodness around her. She welcomed the visiting shepherds and listened intently as they told her about the angels and heavenly hosts appearing from Heaven and proclaiming Jesus as God's Son. Luke 2:15–19 records it like this:

> When the angels had left them and gone into heaven, the shepherds said to one another, "Let's go to Bethlehem and see this thing that has happened, which the Lord has told us about." So they hurried off and found Mary and Joseph, and the baby, who was lying in the manger. When they had seen him, they spread

the word concerning what had been told them about this child, and all who heard it were amazed at what the shepherds said to them. But Mary treasured up all these things and pondered them in her heart.

Isn't that amazing? Mary—young and inexperienced, pregnant out of wedlock, misunderstood, simple, yet devout in her faith. Mary—mother of the Savior of the World—somehow got past her own insecurities, her pain, her frustration, and the chaos all around her, and she didn't try to measure up. That wasn't the call God placed on her and inside of her. Instead, she chose to faithfully do what God asked her to do, and all the while, she treasured up God's goodness in her midst.

I love this story because it gives us a glimpse of Mary's heart as a mother. I'm sure she was scared and unsure of her surroundings, but I also believe that God gave her a true peace that surpassed her understanding. In the midst of all the animal sounds and smells around her—all the exhaustion, all the pressure that would come with birthing and raising the Savior of the World—she chose to treasure the moment.

As beautiful and amazing as that is, this isn't the only time the Bible mentions Mary "treasuring up." Later in Luke 2, we learn that Mary and Joseph lost track of twelve-year-old Jesus during a festival in Jerusalem. This was the Passover festival, where there would have been thousands of people. As the story goes, Mary and Joseph didn't even realize that Jesus was missing until he had been gone an entire day! Can you imagine? To their credit, they were most likely managing a lot of kids within the very chaotic streets of Jerusalem and trying to make the trek back home.

Once they realized that Jesus wasn't with them, they began to panic just like any other parents would. They thought He was among the many relatives and friends who were making the journey with them, but He wasn't. I am sure they were worried sick. When they couldn't find him, they turned around and rushed back to Jerusalem, only to find Jesus studying with the teachers at the temple—safe and calm.

It was in that very moment of finally finding Jesus, enveloped in relief and a whole mixture of emotions, that Mary "treasured up all these things in her heart." She didn't dwell on the fact that they had lost the Savior of the World for three whole days or worry about what others might think about them as parents. She didn't hold on to anger against Jesus for creating this panic in them by choosing to stay behind all by himself. She didn't allow thoughts of insecurity or failure to take residence in her mind and heart.

Mary didn't focus on trying to measure up to someone else's standard, or even her own for that matter. Once again, she chose to *treasure up* God's goodness around her. She chose to be thankful for finding Jesus safe and sound. She even chose to see Jesus' desire to learn from the teachers and be in the temple as a sign of great maturity. I imagine Mary beaming with pride and tearing up as she listened to Jesus ask the teachers questions and grow in knowledge (once her mama bear heart had calmed down a bit, of course). It's like she saw the very first glimpse of God's power and wisdom trickling out of her precious Son. You bet she treasured up every single drop of that goodness.

Mary was actively living out what the apostle Paul teaches the Philippians (and ultimately us) years after Jesus' death and resurrection. In Philippians 4:8–9, he writes, "Finally, brothers and sisters, whatever is true, whatever is noble, whatever is right, whatever is pure, whatever is lovely, whatever is admirable—if anything is excellent or praiseworthy—think about such things...and the God of peace will be with you."

Whenever we make it our mission to look for moments that are true, noble, right, pure, lovely, admirable, excellent, and worthy of praise, we will find God's treasure in our lives. It's the "gold" that we can mentally and emotionally gather up in our mind and heart. God's treasure is always eternal. It's the only kind of treasure that we can take to the grave. It can't be stolen from us; it can only be shared and passed on to our loved ones. It's that sweet moment when your child looks you in the eye and says, "I love you." It's holding your child close as his eyes become heavy and watching him fall asleep. It's seeing the sparkle in your daughter's eyes as she dances in the kitchen. It's praying with your children to accept Jesus as their Lord and Savior, and watching them walk into the waters of baptism. It's trusting God with your child's future, praying until your knees are sore, and finally seeing God answer those prayers after a long season of waiting. It's a husband and wife choosing to fight for their marriage and surrendering their pain to the Lord. It's breakthrough. It's love. It's hope. It's broken hearts made whole again. It's dead things brought to life again. It's old things made new again.

Jesus talks about this kind of treasure in Matthew 6:19–20 when He says, "Do not store up for yourselves treasures on earth, where moths and vermin destroy, and where thieves break in and steal. But store up for yourselves treasures in heaven, where moths and vermin do not destroy, and where thieves do not break in and steal."

God's treasure is eternal. We can't put a price tag on it; it's priceless. It's the kind of treasure that we don't have to and can't steal from someone else, because God is not a thief and would never ask us to do something against His character. This treasure—this gold—is a gift from the Lord that is ours for the taking, yet so many times, we don't reach out and grab it because we are paralyzed by our pain. We question God's goodness and His plan. We can't see past our own failures. We forget about God's promises and how far He has brought us. We aim for perfection only to fall short time and time again, when all God has asked us to do is be faithful.

Sweet Mama, no matter what you are feeling in this moment, no matter how frustrated you are and how much you think you or your kids have ruined the day, please know that God loves you. Resist those defeating thoughts that you will never measure up as a mom. Those are lies straight from the enemy. God calls you His beloved child (John 1:12). His daughter (2 Cor.6:18). A masterpiece (Eph. 2:10). You measure up because *He* made you. When it comes to being the mom God created you to be, He wants you to try to treasure up His goodness in every situation. You must choose to stay *resolute* to your calling as a mom, remain *receptive*—physically, mentally, and emotionally—to your children, and be *resilient* as you process change, disappointments, and frustrations in your parenting journey. The more you actively strive to stay resolute, receptive, and resilient in your calling as a Christ-follower and mother, the more peace you will experience in your heart and home, and you will have a greater capacity to treasure up God's goodness all around you and keep a peace-filled perspective. This doesn't mean that you won't continue to face hard things, but it does mean that you will *never* face them alone. Your mind and heart will become accustomed to seeking out and finding the best kind of treasure there is—the sticky-sweet gifts and moments from God that He has placed in your life.

Dear Lord,

Thank You for giving us the gift of motherhood. We don't take this calling on our lives lightly. Sometimes, we feel overwhelmed by it because we know we aren't perfect. Remind us that You don't ask for perfection; You only ask for our devotion to You and what You have called us to do. Thank You for helping us every step of the way. Help us to look for the "gold"—those sweet moments of Your goodness—in our lives every day. We love You, Lord.

In Jesus' name,
Amen

CHAPTER NINE

Mary, Adorned in Faithfulness

Key Principle: Our conscious and continuous faithfulness to the task of motherhood is our armor against the peace pirates.

When I was growing up in the 1990s, I attended an amazing youth group at Southland Christian Church in Lexington, Kentucky. There we would sing "Take My Life" by Scott Underwood, one of my favorite worship songs. We sang it in the pews, around campfires, and on buses. I loved that song, and its message about faithfulness—that it's what I need and what God wants from from me—truly resonated with me and still does to this day. Faithfulness is something that I long for and need, but I can't be faithful to God and His will without surrendering my heart to Him, trusting Him to form it as He sees fit, and believing that God's plan is better than my own. This is much easier said than done, but just like the angel Gabriel told Mary, "For nothing will be impossible with God" (Luke 1:37 ESV). Nothing, friend. Let that sink in for a minute.

If Mary—a young, naïve, inexperienced woman—can faithfully trust and fulfill the Lord's high calling to carry and give birth to the Savior of the World, then we can also be faithful in our walk with the Lord and our calling as a mother. We need only to surrender our heart and home to Him every day and faithfully love God and our family. One prayer at a time. One step after another in the right direction. We remain faithful by "adorning" ourselves in faithfulness. In Isaiah 11:5, the prophet Isaiah is describing Jesus and says, "Righteousness will be his belt and faithfulness the sash around his waist." Jesus adorned Himself in faithfulness, but what does "faithfulness" really mean and how do we adorn ourselves in it? As I studied the biblical meaning of faithfulness, I learned that the original Hebrew word is *emunah*, which has several meanings, including "firmness, securely fixed in place." Since I am fascinated by Ancient Hebrew word pictures, I decided to dig a little deeper and study the word picture for "faithfulness." What I found astonished me. The Ancient Hebrew word picture for "faithfulness" is:

And here is the meaning of each individual word picture:

look, reveal, breath (a man pointing)

continue (a seed)

secure, add, hook (a tent peg)

chaos (water)

strong, power, leader (an ox head, strong animal)

Fascinating, right? When we consider the meaning of each individual word picture, we gain a greater understanding of what faithfulness entails. We must strive to calmly focus on God, stay strong and secure in Him and His plan, even in the presence of chaos. I love that. As I was studying these word pictures, I found something even more interesting. I found the word picture for "mother." It looks like this:

I couldn't believe it! The Ancient Hebrew word picture for "mother" is an actual part of the word picture for "faithfulness." Go figure! So when you look at the meanings of the individual word pictures for "mother," they depict strength and leadership in the midst of chaos. As I looked a little closer, I learned that the original Hebrew word for "mother" is *eym*, which is defined as "One who fulfills the role of a mother. Maternal tenderness and affection." When I read more about what the ox head word picture stands for, I learned that the ox was a strong animal that both nourished and often provided leather for the people. It was also often used in sacrifices for atonement in Ancient Hebrew times. As I thought more about this, it struck me how fitting this is to describe a mother. We are strong and mighty, yet tender. We strive to lead our kids to Jesus with both authority and affection. We aim to nourish their minds and bellies, and we make sure our kids are clothed and safe. We make great sacrifices along the way to give the best of ourselves to our families. We make it our mission to do all these things regardless of the throes of the day. We make mistakes because we aren't perfect, not one of us. But we get the job done.

As mothers, we often do what we need to do. We remain faithful to the task, and that is awesome. However, we can't do it all on our own, and when we try to do it, we only end up defeated and depleted of God's peace and His perspective. The peace pirates come sailing in and invade our mothership—weigh us down, wear us out, and waste our time. Sweet Mama, we can't let that happen. We must fight back. When we adorn ourselves in faithfulness—to God and our families—we arm ourselves for the battle. Our minds and hearts are focused on God and His promises. We rely on Him as our greatest source of strength, and we rest in Him when we know we need a break. Resting doesn't mean retreating. Friend, we need rest so desperately, and I am not just talking about some shut-eye here. We need a moment for our minds and hearts to have a brief reprieve. For me, this is often having a sweet moment with my husband or a cup of coffee with a friend. Dave and I know how important this is to our relationship and the dynamic of our family, and we do our best to make this a regular part of our weekly routine. This can be difficult at times, but we try to budget the time and money to do so as much as we can. However, I know that Dave can't be my sole source of adult conversation and connection. There is something so special about meeting with other moms and sharing what's going in our lives, marriages, kids, and jobs. We need each other!

After moving halfway across the country this summer, I have been reminded of the great importance that friendship plays in our lives—especially as mothers. We desperately need women in our life who we can relate to and people who embrace us just as we are. I have moved before, and I know that true friendships take time to develop. But I forgot how awkward this can be. I've honestly felt like I'm in middle school all over again in some ways, and I hate it. I know "hate" is a strong word, and it's not one that I use regularly. I just wish I didn't feel so awkward and emotionally fragile—just like I felt in middle school— which I would consider some of the hardest years of my life, if I'm being honest. Instead of feeling inadequate because I couldn't perform a back handspring yet, or didn't have boobs, or didn't wear the right makeup, or didn't own the right Express or Abercrombie jeans, or whatever, I have felt less than enough in other ways some of you might be able to relate to as well. This season has rocked me a bit and messed with my peace.

These days, I'll be talking to a fellow mom who seems excited to make a new friend, only to see her eyes *lose* their sparkle the minute I jokingly say that my kids drive me crazy sometimes, or that I allow my kids to drink Coke on occasion, or that some of my boys aren't currently in organized sports, or...you name it. Normally, this kind of thing wouldn't bother me, but again, I feel so vulnerable and exposed right now due to my heartfelt need to connect with other moms. I just want to find "my people" here where I live, and it's proven to be more difficult than I could ever imagine. Honestly, I think it has made this season of motherhood a little harder for me in some ways, and on particularly hard days, it has caused me to doubt my decisions as a mom and made me feel less equipped for the task.

Why do we do this to each other? Why do we tend to alienate each other based on the most ridiculous things—whether purposely or passively? I honestly could not care less if someone lets their kids drink soft drinks or if they stick only to colorless, organic beverages. Can't we still find some common ground and be friends?

Isn't being fellow mothers enough common ground?

Isn't loving Jesus even *more* common ground?

I sure think so. In fact, I enjoy being friends with lots of different kinds of people, because I can learn something from each and every one of them. I'm not looking for my clone. I'm looking for friends who are authentic, honest, encouraging, motivating, and fun. I want to mean all those things for my friends, too.

Do you feel me, Sweet Mama? Are you longing to connect with some mom friends with whom you can share your motherhood journey? Maybe you already have a good group of mom friends, and you know how valuable these connections truly are in your life. That is awesome. We all can benefit from having a close-knit mama tribe. We need a friend who won't be quick to judge our mothering skills just because our teenage son came to church with greasy hair and a shirt that was two sizes too small one Sunday. We need friends who get it, because honestly, the teenage struggle is real! We need a friend who won't avoid us at our child's elementary school because our young daughter rang the doorbell five times just trying to see if her kids might want to come out and play. Multiple rings might be a bit annoying, but a real friend will avoid the cold shoulder treatment and give a mom (and a kid, for that matter) another chance. We need a friend who will lovingly call us out when we are constantly ranting on about our husband never picking up his laundry or being like so-and-so's husband. We need a friend who listens well and speaks the truth. We need a friend who urges us to get the help we need for ourselves and for our children whether it be Christian counseling, occupational therapy, speech therapy, behavioral therapy, or other treatments or medications. We need a friend who doesn't act like or even believe that she has it all together and all figured out, but who knows that she worships and serves a God who does. We need a friend who always points us to Jesus, and we need to *be* that friend, too.

This dry season of friendship during our move has given me fresh eyes for those who feel left out and misunderstood. I've always considered myself an "includer," but apparently God thought I needed a refresher course. He was right. He always is. God always knows where we need to grow, but real growth requires some level of discomfort. This truth that I am learning reminds me of my own growing pains that I felt in my legs as a kid. I would often experience throbbing aches and pain in my legs at night, and my parents would always comfort me by saying, "The pain will pass, Ashley. Just remember that this is a *good* thing. Those aches and pains mean that you are growing taller and stronger."

Even though my heart might be aching to make new friends and it's painful to see others connecting around me while I feel a bit left out and misunderstood, I know that God is growing me through this. He's molding me into a better friend and a faithful includer. He's reminding me of how important it is to keep fostering friendships near and far, and that every true friend is a blessing straight from the Lord—not to be taken for granted. He's also teaching me to be patient and open.

What about you? Have you felt the sting of loneliness when trying to make friends in a new place or during a new season of life? If so, please know that you are not alone. There is nothing "wrong" with you. You will find *your* people. Keep praying and keep putting yourself out there in social situations and be friendly to those around you even when it feels a bit awkward. You never know when you will meet a kindred spirit and develop a lasting friendship. For those of you who are reading this and are in a sweet season of friendship, I just want to say that we celebrate with you. I, too, know the sheer joy that we experience when we feel like our friends "get us," and we can just be ourselves, laugh, and do life with our people. It's truly a gift. Now, more than ever before, I realize this. But I have also learned how tremendously important it is for us to choose to be includers instead of hovering in our own circles.

Let's always be open to making new friends while always treasuring our older friendships as well. It could make all the difference in the world to a fellow mom. You could be that one friend who finally makes her feel settled in a new place. You could be that one person who reminds her that God made her amazingly unique and awesome and fun to be around. You could help to lessen the blow of her tough transition. You could remind her that she is a great mother and that her kids are great, too. You could be that friend who leaves chicken noodle soup and a blanket on her doorstep when her family has been stuck at home with the flu. You could turn her loneliness to laughter just by including her and being kind. Better yet, *you* could make a great new friend for life. Enough with this middle-aged middle-school stuff. Who wants to go through that again anyway? Instead, let's be the kind of friend that we all so desperately long to have and keep—the kind of friend who helps us to stand firm in our faith and calling as a mother and who brings us more peace and perspective.

A few years ago, our son Chandler, just three years old, ended up breaking his knee in a trampoline incident. We had to take him to the orthopedist to get a full leg cast that he had to wear for four weeks. At that time, our older boys were ten and eight, and our youngest was just a baby. When the orthopedist told me that Chandler shouldn't walk on his leg for all of those weeks, I honestly almost fell over. I asked the doctor if he was going to give Chandler a little wheelchair for him to get around. He told me that he was too young for that. I almost lost my marbles. I mean, how was he supposed to get around? I was nursing an infant. Chandler had preschool every day. This incident was totally throwing a wrench in our normal routine, and my sanity was fragile. The clenching control peace pirate was having a heyday with me.

As we exited the hospital, I loaded the baby and Chandler into our sit-and-stand stroller and backed out of the room—trying not to bang Chandler's hard, green, full-leg cast on the walls. It stuck straight out and made sitting comfortably in the stroller almost impossible. As we made our way to the parking lot, I started to cry. I was tired and weary already, and spending long days—for *four weeks*—with a needy, nursing baby and a very active toddler, who was restricted from walking and doing his normal activities, was going to test my peace and patience for sure.

I called my husband at work and told him the news. He immediately came home and tried to get all of us settled. It was truly an all-hands-on-deck situation. Chandler was in pain, and he felt so frustrated by the cast. Friend, I realize that there are much worse things that a family can go through, but those first few days of this were miserable for us. I prayed every day that God would give me peace and patience, and He did. However, my husband had to go back to work, and the weight of our situation really got to me. I felt so overwhelmed. I put a little post on Facebook about what happened to Chandler including a little video of him trying to crawl around like a little spider with his awkward cast. A few minutes after I posted it, a dear friend of mine, Jenny, texted me and asked if she could come over for a bit and visit. We had been cooped up for the last several days, so I was elated to have the company.

Within an hour, Jenny showed up at my door with a huge bag full of goodies. She brought all kinds of games and activities that Chandler could do without walking. How sweet is that? She brought some Play-Doh with cookie cutters to make shapes. She brought some shaving cream and food coloring for him to play with. He loved that! She brought stickers, coloring books, and books that made noises. For the next several hours, Jenny and I had coffee and talked, and Chandler was the happiest he had been in days. It did my heart so much good, and I will never forget her thoughtfulness and generosity. Jenny brought peace to my heart and home that day, and I will forever be grateful for her friendship.

That special time with my friend softened my heart, lightened my load, refocused my mind, and helped me to remain faithful to my calling as a mom, and it took Chandler's mind off his injury for a while and let him have some fun. God prompted Jenny to help a friend. She was faithful to the task, and Chandler and I were blessed because of her faithfulness.

God reminded me that Godly friends make all the difference in this season of motherhood. Mary knew this truth as well. Even though Elizabeth was her cousin, she was also one of Mary's closest and most faithful friends, and Mary was the same for her. After Gabriel gave Mary her big news and told her that Elizabeth was already with child after not being able to conceive for years, the Bible says that she "hurried" (Luke 1:39) to Judea to see

Elizabeth. When Mary arrived and greeted her, Elizabeth's baby jumped for joy in her womb as she was filled with the Holy Spirit (Luke 1:41), and according to Luke 1:42–45, Elizabeth exclaimed, "Blessed are you among women, and blessed is the child you will bear! But why am I so favored, that the mother of my Lord should come to me? As soon as the sound of your greeting reached my ears, the baby in my womb leaped for joy. Blessed is she who has believed that the Lord would fulfill his promises to her!"

What a faithful and faith-filled friend! According to the Word, Mary spent three months with Elizabeth as Jesus grew inside her own womb, and many biblical scholars believe Mary was there for the birth of Elizabeth's baby, who later became known as John the Baptist. I love reading about this deep and true friendship because I think it illustrates the important role that friendship plays in our lives as mothers. Not only was Mary there for Elizabeth during her much-anticipated pregnancy and birth, but I am sure that Elizabeth was also a great confidante for Mary during her miraculous pregnancy that she surely knew would be widely misunderstood and judged. I imagine Mary having waves of joy and fear in those days. I am sure there were moments of tears. I picture Elizabeth, a loving and faithful friend, praying over Mary and reassuring her that God keeps his promises. I can see her taking Mary's hand and placing it on her belly saying, "Mary, do you feel that kick? Do you remember all those years we prayed together for this child? Zechariah and I waited and believed that God would give us the desire of our hearts. Look at what God did! This child is a miracle that brings us great joy. The child in your womb will not only bring you and Joseph joy, but He will bring joy and peace to the entire world for generations to come!"

That is the kind of friendship Mary and Elizabeth had and the kind of friendships that we all need. They encouraged one another to stay the course and keep the faith. In Ephesians 6:14–15, Paul writes, "Stand firm then, with the belt of truth buckled around your waist, with the breastplate of righteousness in place, and with your feet fitted with the readiness that comes from the gospel of peace." Remember, the true meaning of faithfulness is to stand firm, and Godly friends encourage us to stand back up when we fall, help us to regain our footing, and point us to the Lord and His plan for our life. They encourage us to stay faithful with their words and their example. They share their testimony of God's faithfulness in their own lives. They help to bring order where there is chaos. Godly friends pursue, promote, and protect peace in their own hearts and homes, and they influence their friends and family to do the same. True friends urge one another to treasure up God's goodness around them and even share it with one another.

Truth is, we become like the people we hang around the most, and we need to have an inner circle of friends who desire God's peace and pursue it as much, if not more, than we do. If they don't value His peace in their own lives, then they are not going to encourage us to value it in our own lives. Please don't misunderstand me. It's good to have a variety of friends, but as mamas who want to follow Jesus and have God's peace in our lives, we need our closest friendships to be with other Christ-followers. They have a great influence in our life when it comes to our perspective, and we need friends who make us better, not bitter. We need friends who point to the truth of God's Word, not their mere opinion or what's socially acceptable.

Friend, we keep the peace pirates at bay by protecting our minds through learning and accepting the truth of His Word, guarding our hearts by not allowing shame or discouragement to linger there, and choosing to be at peace regardless of our circumstances, knowing that God is always in control. Godly friends help us to stay vigilant in the pursuit, promotion, and protection of peace. We need to make it our mission to *find* those friends and to *be* that friend. When our mind is focused on God, the forgiveness we have through Christ, and remain faithful to the calling He has placed on our lives, we will have the peace of mind and heart to treasure up God's goodness no matter what circumstance we are facing.

A prayer for those longing for faithfulness:

Dear Lord,

Thank You for being a faithful God. You never ask us to do something that You haven't already demonstrated for us. Help us to remain faithful to You and the tasks You have given us as mothers and Christ-followers. When we are weary, give us strength, Lord. When we lose our way, remind us to focus on You and take it one step at a time. We want to stay on the peaceful path and treasure up Your goodness all along the way.

In Jesus' name,
Amen

CHAPTER TEN

Bowing to the Throne of Faithfulness

Key Principle: We mother best when we fully surrender our hearts and even our children to the Lord and allow His perfect peace to guard our hearts and minds.

A few years ago, our precious guinea pig named "Brave" passed away. The children gave her that name because she was the only piggie that didn't run away from our rambunctious boys at the pet store. That day we went to Petco, our boys smashed their faces against the glass of their cages and watched most of the piggies squeal and run for their lives to the other side. But not the one with a strawberry-blond streak across her back. She was different. She made her way toward the boys and sniffed the glass, as if she could smell their excitement. Who knows? Maybe she could. Our then youngest, Chandler, squealed and said,

"She likes us! Can we get her, Mom and Dad?" How could we refuse? We took her home that day and had her for years.

After around four years, we began to notice her aging and not acting like her energetic, squealy self, and we were all well aware of her impending death. When I came home and saw her lifeless body nestled up next to her little edible play hut, I felt the finality of our time with her. It hit me harder than I'd expected. My heart sank, and I started bawling. I cried and cried as I thought about how I was going to tell our then nine-year-old, Connor, who had always played with her and fed her carrots every day. She was our boys' first and only pet. The boys loved her—especially Connor. She had been the center of attention at the boys' birthday parties, and she was a neighborhood celebrity among the kids. We bathed her, got special veggies and toys for her, and gave her frequent back massages to hear her sweet guinea pig purr. Most of all, we just loved her.

I waited on the front porch for Connor to get off the bus. All I could do was stare at him off in the distance, and I prayed that God would give me the right words as he came closer. At one point, he smiled and yelled, "Hi, Mommy!" I waved at him and told him to come to me. His facial expression changed when he saw that I had been crying. When he asked me what was wrong, I told him that Brave had passed away. He quickly ran to her cage to see her. He reached down to touch her and felt how stiff her body had become. Tears began streaming down his face, and he put his arms around me as he cried. He was heartbroken as we prepared to bury her little body in the backyard.

My husband gathered the kids and said the Twenty-Third Psalm as he laid her down in her burial spot beside our trampoline. He talked about Brave being a sweet pet, and we each shared our favorite memory of her. Through his tears, Connor talked about how much fun he had with Brave and ended with saying, "I think Brave had a good life. I think she was a happy guinea pig with us." I think he was right. Connor placed a special stone on top of the grave, and that was it. Brave is now a treasured-up memory—a very special childhood pet.

That night, I talked to my husband about Brave, and once again, I couldn't help but cry. I even told my husband that I didn't understand why Brave's death had been so upsetting to me. He gave me the most compassionate look as I ugly-cried over Brave, and said, "Ashley, I think you are sad that Brave passed away, but I think you're also sad about the reality that a part of their childhood has passed, too."

I had never thought about it that way, but he was right. As parents, we get up every day and do what needs to be done. It's so easy to get lost in the busyness and daily grind of it all, but *every now and then, God gives us little reminders that this life is short and childhood is fleeting.* The older my kids get, the clearer this is to me. I don't want to rush it. Sometimes, I wish time would just slow down, but unfortunately, it can't. It keeps ticking on with or without our approval. Only God knows the number of our days. We don't have a say in that. *What we can do is pause and treasure it up—the happy moments and the sad ones. We need to acknowledge what has passed so we can truly embrace what's ahead.* We tried our best to do that with Brave's passing. I know this will not be the last pet that we bury or the last time that my kids experience grief, but I do know that this was a moment that we will never forget. Brave's passing brought our family together for a moment of reflection not only on what she meant to us, but also on the sweet childhood memories that were made during her four years with us. For that, I am grateful.

We all have a story and a struggle, and each of us will experience a life full of highs and lows, twists and turns. Life as we know it can be so amazingly grand, and then it can suddenly take a tragic detour that turns everything upside down, leaving us scared, confused, and desperate for hope. Sometimes I can't help but ask God why He allows so many tragedies to occur, but the longer I live, the more I see that He uses tragedy to teach us some powerful truths that can only be learned by walking through these painful experiences.

Recently, my heart has broken for so many of my friends who have experienced some of life's greatest tragedies. Not long ago, my friend's thirty-seven-year-old brother had a heart attack and passed away suddenly while mowing his lawn. His wife, children, family, and friends are still processing and mourning this great loss. One of my girlfriends was recently diagnosed with cancer after a routine Pap smear. She had to have an emergency hysterectomy at the young age of thirty-three. Thankfully, she is now cancer-free, but she is still required to attend routine check-ups every six months for several years just to make sure the cancer doesn't return. None of us expects to get a sobering diagnosis or a phone call that our loved one has passed away, but it can happen to any of us.

I have had many friends share about their struggles. No story or struggle has affected me more than this one. Although I haven't seen my childhood friend Katie Anne in years or even met her husband and two beautiful girls, and precious baby boy, I can't help but think about their family every single day. You see, two weeks after she gave birth to her second baby girl, Katie Anne received the absolutely devastating news that her two-year-old daughter, Bennett, had an aggressive form of brain cancer. In an instant, their lives were turned upside down, and they had to face one of the most difficult and heart-rending journeys that any parent can experience. They moved their whole lives to the children's hospital and began treatments immediately. Playdates, family time at the pool, bubble baths, lunch out with friends, and weekly date nights came to a screeching halt. Life had to be drastically different for the foreseeable future; they had to fight—with every fiber of their being— to save their daughter's precious life.

When I first received the news via a CaringBridge.com post on Facebook, I felt sick to my stomach. So many questions flooded my mind like:

Oh my goodness, what is going to happen to this little girl?

What if this happened to our family?

How are Katie Anne and her husband, Billy, going to get through all of this . . . and with a newborn?

Why do these awful things happen, especially to precious, innocent children?

There was a part of me that didn't want to read about the details in her posts so my mind and heart wouldn't have to go there, but I decided to read them anyway. I read every single post and kept this family in my prayers every day. Katie Anne shared her heart and soul in each post. She talked about the good things, like extended time together and special gestures from friends, and the horrific things, like watching her daughter lose her beautiful hair and the terrible fits that Bennett would throw because of all the needles, surgeries, and vomiting. Every post I read brought me to tears. I admired Katie Anne's willingness to be so raw with her feelings and emotions, but the thing that moved me the most was her amazingly strong faith in God. It wasn't a flowery, singsong kind of faith. It had grit. It was rock solid, honest, and assured. In every post, it was evident that she firmly believed in the power of prayer and that God was still in control even in the worst of circumstances.

I remember reading one of Katie Anne's posts that brought me to my knees in sadness, and I can only imagine how she must have felt hearing the news. She shared that after multiple rounds of chemotherapy and surgeries, Bennett's brain tumors had grown and even multiplied. The doctors offered a variety of next steps, but none were without severe lasting side effects, and the effectiveness was deemed minimal. Katie Anne said she and Billy had been praying that God would make the next steps crystal clear for them, and they took this devastating news as an answer to prayer. It certainly wasn't the answer they wanted, but it did give them more clarity. They decided to move back home and enjoy sweet Bennett without continuing any treatments. Katie Anne acknowledged how scared she was and how she didn't want to think about the fleeting time they had with Bennett, but she was thankful to experience being a family at home once again.

In the months that followed, Katie Anne and Billy treasured up every moment they had with Bennett. They had to mostly stay at home due to Bennett's declining health, but they didn't let that get them down and keep them from seeing God's goodness in their precious little girl. At first, Katie Anne would give her friends and family a glimpse of their sweet time at home with Facebook videos of her and Bennett being silly and singing together and lots of pictures of them cuddling with her. Understandably, Katie Anne started posting less and less on Facebook to soak in more time with her little girl.

Then, on a sunny autumn day, Katie Anne put a post on CaringBridge.com that she and her family had been dreading. Bennett had finally gone to be with Jesus, in her own home and with her family there beside her. Katie Anne shared that she had asked God to make Bennett's passing a peaceful one, and she believed that He answered that prayer. Katie Anne wrote about what a fighter Bennett had been and how thankful they were to have had the time they'd had with their beautiful daughter. She also thanked the doctors, hospital staff, and the people at the Ronald McDonald House, where they had spent some months.

My heart broke for Katie Anne, her husband, and the rest of their family with every word I read.

Friend, as I write about this, tears are welling up in my eyes. It all seems so unfair. Bennett was only four years old. *Four. Years. Old.* As a mother, I can only imagine how Katie Anne must feel. After all of this . . . after all the fits, the needles, the surgeries, the "what ifs," the "this might work" responses, the endless vomiting, the scans, the reevaluations, the weight loss, the sunken eyes, the loss of spunk, the time away, the tears, the fears, the anger, the close calls, the sleepless nights, the mounting medical bills, and all the things that come with this ugly, hideous cancer . . . only to say good-bye to your precious baby girl. It's so deeply heartbreaking. It's messy. There is no explanation—no answer—nothing I can say to make it better. Oh, how I wish I could. There is one thing, however, that cancer can't take away from this family. That one thing is *love*. Love never gives up. Love never fails. Love remains. God is the very embodiment of love. He is still there with them. Bennett is with Him—without any cancer, or pain, or fear. He loves her, and He certainly loves this family.

So in the midst of all this heartache and gut-wrenching news, what is it that tragedy can really teach us?

1. **God promises that something good will rise from the ashes of our pain.** When processing these horrendous situations, I can't help but cling to Romans 8:28, "And we know that in all things God works for the good of those who love him, who have been called

according to his purpose." I don't believe God causes cancer, but I do know that He promises to use *all* things for good. He will not waste our tears, disappointments, losses, and struggles. He will use them for good.

2. **We can be strong in all circumstances, with God's help.** After reading all of Katie Anne's posts, I have seen one of my favorite verses lived out again and again: "Be strong and courageous. Do not be afraid or terrified because of them, for the LORD your God goes with you; he will never leave you nor forsake you" (Deut. 31:6). Katie Anne and Billy are the very definition of "strong and courageous." I have seen them hold on to the promise that God will "never leave us or forsake us" with all of their might. I have a deeper understanding of this verse because of this family and their willingness to share their heart-rending journey. I am challenged by their strong faith amid the most helpless and hardest of circumstances.

3. **We need each other.** When we get news that a friend is facing a devastating circumstance of any kind, let's not look away to shield ourselves from entering into their pain. Let's allow ourselves to share in their burden. Galatians 6:2 says, "Carry each other's burdens, and in this way you will fulfill the law of Christ." In many of her posts, Katie Anne so graciously thanked all of the people who had been praying for them and asked them for their continued prayers. Around Christmastime, she also stated that Bennett loved seeing the three thousand cards they received. She showed her appreciation for the love that was shown, and she

said it raised their spirits. That is what we are called to do as those engaging in another's difficult journey. We help to carry the burden in whatever way we can. We *can't* explain their difficult situation or lift the pain, but we *can* pray for them, bring them a meal, watch their children, offer to clean their house, or offer to help with their medical bills. We can be a blessing in a time of great need.

4. **Life is too short and unpredictable to sweat the small stuff.** When I think about all the hardship that Katie Anne and her family have been through, it reminds me of how ridiculous and insignificant my daily gripes truly are. It has caused me to hug my kids a little tighter, not to get so bent out of shape when they break something, and to view every "Mommy, sit by me" or "Mommy, look at this" as the most beautiful soundtrack in my life right now. This couple has shown me that there are more moments to treasure up than I even realize. I just need to look a little closer to find them. Their story has opened my eyes to the needs of families facing childhood cancer and how we can help. More than anything, Bennett's story has reminded me that each day is a precious gift to be treasured and lived out to the fullest.

Tragedy can certainly touch us and teach us, if we allow it to. Pain is something that we must process, and it can bring us closer to the Lord. First, we must surrender to Him. Many times, we try to hold on to our pain and process it by ourselves. However, we can't find healing when we are isolated in the darkness. That is when pain becomes a pitfall for our peace. And the enemy would love nothing more than to keep us there and have the peace pirates plunder every ounce of peace in our heart and home. God tells us to bring Him our pain. To lay it at His feet. To let Him carry our burden. To allow Him to heal our hearts and home.

God offers us purpose when we bring our pain to Him and lay it at His feet. We must let go and allow Him to heal us so that our hands, hearts, and homes can be ready for the good He is going to bring us. In the years that followed Bennett's death, I watched from afar as Katie Anne did this. In the days prior to Bennett's death, they knew that she was fading, and Katie Anne believed that she needed to prepare her daughter for the day she would meet Jesus and go to Heaven. Katie Anne didn't want Bennett to be afraid, so she told her everything she knew about Heaven. She told her how she wouldn't have to go to the hospital anymore or have any pain. She told her she would meet Jesus and give Him a big hug. She told her how the angels would sing so gloriously, and she told her that there would be field upon field of beautiful flowers in Heaven. In one conversation, Bennett said, "Mommy, I am going to send you flowers from Heaven." A teary-eyed Katie Anne responded with, "Oh, Bennett, I would love that!"

A few months after Bennett passed away, Katie Anne and her husband were rolling up a rug so they could clean their hardwood floors. As they picked up the rug, a puzzle piece fell out. Katie Anne thought this was odd because they had never owned a puzzle. She went to pick it up and throw it away, but when she turned the puzzle piece over, her heart skipped a beat. She couldn't believe what she saw. This lone little puzzle piece had one white flower on it, perfectly placed in the middle. Katie Anne remembered the promise that Bennett had made to her, and she looked up and thanked God for helping Bennett to fulfill her promise. Katie Anne knew God was sending her treasure from Heaven with this little flower on a puzzle piece.

As I read Katie Anne's beautiful words describing this moment on her CaringBridge.com page, I was so struck by this story. How fitting that the flower was on a puzzle piece of all things, because life is often like a puzzle with a million pieces. We get to take it in only one piece at a time, and we can't see the greater puzzle that God is masterfully constructing. We just need to trust that even when it feels like our life is a mound of puzzle pieces that have fallen apart, our Heavenly Father is carefully placing them all back together. Piece by piece. When we trust Him with the pieces, that's where peace is, and every piece has purpose in His good plan. Every piece has treasure within it.

I love how Paul describes this in his letter to Timothy in 1 Timothy 6:17–19:

Command those who are rich in this present world not to be arrogant nor to put their hope in wealth, which is so uncertain, but to put their hope in God, who richly provides us with everything for our enjoyment. Command them to do good, to be rich in good deeds, and to be generous and willing to share. In this way they will lay up treasure for themselves as a firm foundation for the coming age, so that they may take hold of the life that is truly life.

I think it is by no mistake that Paul uses that same kind of phrasing that Mary had used to tell Luke about the birth of Jesus (and even losing track of twelve-year-old Jesus for three days) decades prior to his letter to Timothy. Yes, Paul is encouraging Christ-followers to do good deeds and lead people to Jesus, but he is also urging them (and us) to keep our minds and hearts focused on storing up the *right* kind of treasure—God's peace, presence, purpose, and providence in our lives. That treasure is eternal, unbreakable, sharable, and immeasurable.

As I mentioned earlier, my husband and I have four sons with a ten-year age range. With so many kiddos in the house, it can be hard to give each one of them the individual focus that he needs, so my husband and I both try to take each boy on a special date every now and then. I want to treasure up every moment that I can. As my two older boys have moved into the double digits, I figured that they wouldn't want "mom time" anymore. Boy, was I wrong.

Years ago, I asked my then ten-year-old, Connor, if he'd like to go on a Connor-Mommy Date, and he quickly said yes. Then, he asked if he could plan the whole thing, and I honestly didn't know what to think. Connor is super-creative. He's my free spirit—part hippie, part monkey, part Pokémon trainer. You get the picture. He's an interesting little dude. So when he asked to plan the date, I really didn't know what he would have in mind. I asked him where he would like to go, and he exclaimed, "The mall!" So off we went.

We started out by walking through the bookstore and looking at funny books. Connor always loves browsing them, and of course, he likes taking a little sneak peek at the Pokémon figures as well. After that, we went and sat in the massage chairs. You know... the ones that have the little shiatsu back massagers that dig in and karate-chop your back all at the same time? We agreed to do it for fifteen minutes. Connor squealed as the little massagers moved up and down his back. He was giggling so loud that the people who walked by couldn't help but smile, and some of them even decided to join us in the chairs next to us. It was so relaxing and fun.

After our massages, Connor wanted to go to the lower level of the mall to ride the motorized stuffed animals. Yes, you read that right, and yes, it's as random and weird as it sounds. Picture an enormous stuffed animal on all fours with wheels underneath its feet. Now, imagine that it has a button that you can push that makes it motor around at about three to five miles an hour. Okay, now, envision yourself hopping on one of these babies and riding it throughout the mall. Yeah. You got it. Embarrassing and awesome all at the same time, and that's what my awesome ten-year-old wanted to do. So we did it.

He hopped on a panda bear, and I saddled up on a moose. When we flipped the switches to get the animals

moving, we quickly noticed that Connor's panda was put-
tering out. So I swapped animals with him, and I scooted
along on his panda while he laughed hysterically. He
laughed so hard that tears came down his face, and I
couldn't help but laugh at myself, too. We looked ridiculous! Okay...*I* was the one who looked ridiculous, but I
didn't care. All I could think about was how blessed I am
to have Connor in my life. What a gift it is to spend time
with him and call him my son. I love his sense of humor
and thirst for adventure. I love his heart to help others and
his tenderness with his crazy little brothers. Our time on
the motorized stuffed animals was fun and silly for Connor, but to me, it was one of those special moments that I
needed to "treasure up" in my heart—like Mary did when
she was raising Jesus.

Mary chose to treasure up moments with young Jesus
no matter what chaos was around her. Mary knew that
those moments—those sweet and fleeting moments of
raising kids through celebrations and heartbreaks—are like
golden treasure. That's exactly what Connor's perfectly
planned mother-son date was for me. Those special moments will forever be treasured up in my mind and heart
like precious gold, and I will gladly ponder them as often
as I can.

Treasuring up God's goodness is something that takes
intentionality and practice. It's especially difficult when
we're defeated and depleted and lacking in peace. That is
precisely why we must fight against the peace pirates and
pursue, promote, and protect God's peace in our heart and
home *every day*. Some days, it's going to feel like a los-

ing battle, but we must keep on fighting and stay faithful. Have you ever had one of those days when you've thought to yourself—or even said out loud—"I. Am. Done!"? I have, and it has kind of been a recurring theme for me during certain seasons of motherhood. Sometimes, I'm exhausted, and I feel like I never have enough time for...well, anything...or anyone, for that matter. But then, the Holy Spirit reminds me of these four simple words: *This, too, shall pass.* That's it. Those four simple words hit my ears like church bells. I remember when I first heard them on a cooking show, of all places, but I felt like God used that statement to remind me that this tireless season of motherhood is passing quickly. These four words are comforting and convicting to me all at the same time.

I was coming off our hectic morning routine of getting our two older boys up, fed, and ready for school right before I heard those words. I had just sat down to sip on—okay, gulp down—some much-needed coffee and was folding mounds of laundry that should've been done days ago. *Sigh.* Our, youngest, then a baby, was crying because he had a dirty diaper. I'd just received a message from the doctor's office stating that if we missed yet *another* appointment, we'd have to be released from their practice. How could we have missed *so many? Seriously?* Then I couldn't find our four-year-old for a minute. I searched the room and saw the front door wide open. *Help me, Lord Jesus.* Just as I started to head out the front door, chasing down my four-year-old who (in his *underwear*) is screaming and crying to go ride his tricycle—I heard those four simple words. Oh, how I needed those words, and I will probably need them tomorrow as well. And the following weeks, months, and years.

Can you relate, Sweet Mama? Are you exhausted? Do you feel overwhelmed? Are you longing for God's peace and maybe a still moment to yourself while also wanting to make sure you don't miss the treasure—the sticky, sweet, messy moments where you see God at work in your life and the lives of your kids? It's the whole reason why you wanted to become a mom in the first place, right? Motherhood is one of the main reasons that God placed you on this earth and in this time and place, correct? It's one of the highest, most exhausting, yet most rewarding callings that God has placed on your life. I get it, friend. The stakes are high. Raising kids is hard, not to mention juggling the many other hats we wear . . . working, keeping a house, cooking dinner, attending activities, volunteering at church, and the list goes on and on.

It's a crazy busy season. But it's crazy beautiful, too, and we can experience God's peace and treasure up God's goodness in the midst of it all. We don't have to settle for being defeated and depleted—feeling like we're missing the mark as a mom, trying to prove our worth as a mother, clenching control of our kids only to feel like a failure, getting trapped in the cycle of comparing ourselves to the highlight reels of other moms on social media, and allowing our expectations to set us up for disappointment and frustration. We don't have to live this way. We must pursue, promote, and protect God's peace in our hearts, and we must fight against the peace pirates. God is with us every step of the way, and as we cling to Him and bow to the throne of faithfulness, He will give us His perfect peace and open our eyes wide to His goodness—His treasure—in our lives.

We may change diaper after diaper, but nothing is better than an involuntary baby giggle while wiping those chubby cheeks. We may be running late in the morning, but extra morning cuddles make it all worth it. Honestly, a missed doctor's appointment can be rescheduled. Or I could get a lot better at writing them all down on a calendar. *Sigh.* It's all about progress, not perfection. Sometimes, we just need a moment to breathe and take in the crazy beautiful, kid-*full* life we have. It doesn't mean we can't acknowledge that much of this season is hard, messy, stressful, and frustrating, but it does mean that we might need to remind ourselves that "this, too, shall pass" before this season is nothing more than a memory.

So treasure it up, Sweet Mama. Take it *all* in. You were made for this.

Here is a prayer for all the peace-seeking mamas longing to treasure up:

Dear Lord,

Thank You for loving me. Thank You for reconciling me to Yourself and giving me freedom through Your Son, Jesus. Thank You for making me a mother and helping me to be the very best mother I can be—a peace-filled, peaceful, and faithful mom. Even when life is difficult and my heart is broken, help me to feel Your presence and know that You are with me. May I experience Your perfect peace that surpasses my understanding and do my best to pursue it, promote it, and protect it in my heart and home. Heavenly Father, open my eyes wide to see all the blessings You have placed in my life—the real golden treasure that is eternal. May I treasure up as much of it as I can and think about it often.

In Jesus' name,
Amen

Acknowledgments

Reader, thank you so much for taking the time to read this book. I hope and pray it continues to be a tremendous blessing to you and brings more peace into your heart and home. This book would not have been possible without my literary agent, Blythe Daniel. Blythe, thank you for pushing me to get this book just right and supporting me through the entire process. I would also like to thank acquisitions editor Keren Baltzer, for catching the vision of this book and taking a chance on me. I am so grateful to the entire team at FaithWords Publishing, and I want to give a special thanks to my editors, Virginia Bhashkar and Tareth Mitch.

I wouldn't have been able to write this book without the support and inspiration of my sweet family. To Mom and Dad, Bill and Mary McCray, thank you for teaching me that I can do anything I put my mind to and telling me to go after my dreams. I love you all. To my in-laws, Brad and Karen Willis, thank you for encouraging me and loving me like your own daughter. Love you. To my sweet husband, Dave, you are my favorite person in the world, and you inspire me every day to be better while also loving me just as I am. You have given me the greatest treasures in my life, and I love that we are on this wild adventure together in raising our four little buccaneers. I love you.

Lastly, but most importantly, I thank God for giving me this opportunity to share the message of His lasting peace with others. Thank You, Lord, for giving us your peace that surpasses understanding. May we all be intentional about pursing it, promoting it, and protecting it, and may we treasure up all the blessings You've placed in our lives each day.

About the Author

Ashley Willis is the author or co-author of seven books and many viral blog articles on issues related to faith, mental health, motherhood, and marriage. Along with her husband, Dave, she co-hosts the popular *Naked Marriage* podcast and the TV program *Marriage Today*. Ashley's resources have provided encouragement, hope, and practical instruction to millions around the world. Ashley and Dave live with their four amazing sons and their spoiled dog "Chi Chi" in Keller, Texas. For additional resources, please visit www.AshleyWillis.org, and follow her on Facebook at www.facebook.com/ashleywillisencouragement.

Ahoy, Mateys! The Willis family.